Knot Crazy

by Clyde Carter

ISBN # 978-0-9827379-4-1
©2014 Clyde Carter - all rights reserved.
Edition 1, Printed in the USA.

Table of Contents

I.   Introduction   1

II.   History of Rope and Knots   3

III. About the Author   4

III. Tips and Rope Selection   5

IV.   Warnings and Safety Tips   6

V.   Basic Terms   7

Section I: Tricks For Tying Practical Knots   9

   1. Overhand Knot   9

     a. Whip a Knot   10

     b. Pop a Knot   11

     c. Roll a Knot   12

     d. Roll a Knot with a Weighted Rope   13

     e. Flip a Knot   14

     f. Drop a Knot   15

     g. Overhand as a Safety Knot   16

     h. Double Overhand as a Safety Knot   17

   2. Slip Knot   18

     a. Whip a Slip   19

   3. Figure Eight   20

     a. Twist an Eight   21

     b. Roll an Eight   22

     c. Whip an Eight   23

     d. Quick Figure Eight   24

     e. Quick Figure Eight on a Bight   25

Table of Contents

4. Square   26

    a. One-Second Square Knot   27

    b. Untying the Square Knot   28

5. Bowline   29

    a. One-Handed Bowline   30

    b. Bowline from a Slip Knot   32

    c. Bowline with a Flip   33

    d. Quick Bowline on a Post   34

    e. Untying the Bowline   35

6. Angler's Loop   36

    a. Quick Angler's Loop   36

    b. Girth Hitching the Angler's Loop   37

7. Clove Hitch   38

    a. Picking up a Clove Hitch   39

    b. Throwing a Clove Hitch - I   40

    c. Throwing a Clove Hitch – II   41

    d. One Hand Clove Hitch   42

    e. One Hand Clove Hitch Clip   43

8. Munter Hitch   44

    a. One Hand Munter   45

9. Fisherman's Knot   46

    a. Quick Fisherman's Knot   46

    b. Quick True Fisherman's Knot   48

10. Double Fisherman's Knot   50

    a. Quick Double Fisherman's Knot   51

11. Fisherman's Loop   52

    a. Quick Fisherman's Loop   53

    b. Quick True Fisherman's Loop I   54

    c. Quick True Fisherman's Loop II   55

Table of Contents

12. Butterfly Knot   56
    a. Quick Butterfly Knot   57
13. Sheet Bend   58
    a. Quick Sheet Bend   59
14. Trucker's Hitch   60
    a. Quick Truckers Knot   61
15. Taut-line Hitch   62
    a. Slippery Taut-line Hitch   63

Section II: Rope Tricks For Fun   65
1. Monkey Chain   66
2. Three Knot Monkey Chain   68
3. Don't Let Go   70
4. Don't Let Go – Figure Eight   72
5. The Real Don't Let Go   74
6. The Jerry Stone Pop a Knot   75
7. Thread the Needle   76
8. Rope (Eskimo) Yo-Yo   78
9. Tom Fool Knot   79
10. Knotted Bow   80
11. Sniff a Rope   82
12. Ghost Fingers   83
    a. Old Sailor's Ghost fingers   84
    b. Figure Eight Ghost Fingers   86
    c. Double Figure Eight Ghost Fingers   88
    d. Captain Hook's Ghost Finger   90
    e. Spinning Hand Ghost Finger   92
    f. Gun Point Ghost Finger   94
    g. Strangled Ghost Finger   95

Table of Contents

h. Ghost Thumb   96

13. Square Knot Cut and Restore   97

14. Double Loop Cut and Restore   98

15. Single Strand Cut and Restore   99

16. Thief Knot   100

17. Dragon Bowline   102

18. Binders Twine Twist   102

Section III: Tricks For Young Children   103

1. Blow a Knot   104

2. Chain Sinnet   105

3. Ghost Arm   106

4. Continuous Loop   106

VI. Final Thoughts   107

VII. Bibliography   108

The year was 1768 when Jonathan Munkhouse signed up to be a midshipman on James Cook's expedition to the South Pacific. The deck hands hoisted the topsails as they left the safety of the Port of Plymouth and headed south toward the Madeira Islands. All hands were busy for about an hour as the captain gave orders and set their course. Once the ship was underway, the men gathered on her deck as Great Britain slowly faded below the horizon. Soon there was nothing in sight but ocean as far as the eye could see.

Ships in those days didn't travel very fast. This expedition was expected to take a couple of years. Between destinations, the sailors were often left with idle time, and of course the technology of today didn't exist. There were no phones, no internet, and no social media—not even cameras. But there was lots of rope lying around. So rope became one means of entertainment. Who could tie the most fancy knots …the quickest knots …or even the trickiest knots? To some, rope became an obsession. Munkhouse was one.

He had been a deck hand for several years and had learned the ropes from the old sailors. On his last voyage to sea, he lost a week's ration of rum to an old sailor who wagered he could tie a simple overhand knot in a short piece of rope without letting go of the ends. After attempting the trick for a half day, Munkhouse deemed it impossible and took the bet. The old sailor crossed his arms in a knot before picking up the ends of the rope; and as he unfolded his arms, the knot formed in the rope (page 74, "The Real Don't Let Go").

Little did the old sailor know the true origin of this trick. It was actually invented by a Chinese monk in the year 300 BC. The monk used it as a riddle to teach his apprentice that many of the answers to life's great questions are found within. A Chinese trader learned the trick by observing the monks, and as he traveled on the Silk Trade Route he shared the trick with others. The trick was passed from one person to another, generation after generation. It found its way to Luoyang and then Niya, to Merv and Antioch. It was eventually picked up by a Turkish sailor who carried it to sea. Well over a thousand years later, the old sailor picked it up on one of his voyages.

Back to Munkhouse… Two days into the voyage he did the same trick on John Bootie, another midshipman. Bootie was so upset that he spent the next several days devising a way to earn his ration back. He came back to Munkhouse with the wager that he could do the same trick without crossing his arms first. Munkhouse knew this was impossible and was up to earning another week's ration of rum, so he took the bet. To his astonishment, Bootie was able to do it (page 70, "Don't Let Go"). Monkhouse couldn't believe his eyes!

In truth, there is no record of this actually happening. This is just one rendition of what might have happened. It is true, however, that rope handlers have devised tricks to their trade over thousands of years. Some of these tricks are quicker or more efficient ways of tying knots and handling rope, and some tricks are just for fun and entertainment.

For 40 years, I have had jobs and recreational pursuits that require work with rope and knots. During this time I've worked with people who have taught me tricks with rope: either to become more efficient, or tricks for fun and entertainment. I've even put my own twist on some of the tricks. The tricks you'll find in this book are my collection. That doesn't mean I invented them. These are just the ones that I've enjoyed and been able to keep in my head through practice. In learning and practicing these tricks, I have gained a much greater appreciation for the skill and craftsmanship behind the activities in which I participate—collective wisdom that has been passed down through the ages. I've learned that knot tying and rope work can be fun. I've also developed a desire to carry on the traditions of knotcraft and pass them on to the people I work with. That is why I wrote this book.

In this age of increasing technology, I hope the traditions of old will be kept alive. Through writing this book, I hope that you will catch the obsession caught by Munkhouse so many years ago!

Anyone who has taken a serious look into the history of knots, including archeologists and anthropologists, tends to agree that cordage and knots were possibly among the first tools used by humans. The need for them arose when humans began to gather food, build shelters, travel, and move their belongings. The need increased when humans began to hunt, trap, fish, make clothing, and take to the water in boats. There is even evidence that cordage and knots were used in the first expressions of art through the creation of necklaces, bracelets, and intricate clothing. Anthropologists also tell of the important role rope and knots played in making meaning out of existence. Knots and cordage often took on a metaphorical, mystical, or even magical meaning in primitive religion, myth, and folklore. If this interests you, I suggest you read the work of the late professor Clarence Day in *The Art of Knotting and Splicing*. Day has given one of most succinct and well-documented accounts that I've found on the history of rope and knots.

Evidence of the earliest knots is sparse because cordage was made of organic fibers and was quick to decay. In the evidence that does exist in the literature and in the few archeological sites where the conditions were right for preservation, the same basic knots show up. In all corners of the globe and all eras of time, you will find Overhands, Figure Eights, Square Knots, Bowlines, and Clove Hitches. These basic knots either spread across the planet with the migration of people, or were invented and reinvented in various parts of the world and over various time periods because they worked and were easy to tie. My guess is it was a combination of both.

As I searched for the origins of the tricks in this book, I couldn't help but feel that they have similar pasts. Knot tricks are scattered through the books found in this book's Bibliography. In most cases, the authors admit these tricks were passed to them by another rope handler. Some of the tricks in this book possibly came from the golden age of sailing, or they may have much deeper roots. Regardless, they have been passed from person to person, culture to culture, and generation to generation by a long line of knot tiers.

These knot tiers and rope handlers included mariners, nomads, traders, truckers, fishermen, ranchers, farmers, whalers, mountaineers, seamstresses, cowboys, magicians, arborists, soldiers, scuba divers, firemen, rescuers, zip liners, Sherpas, kayakers, canoeists, rock climbers, campers, backpackers, mailmen, mule train guides, yak packers, horse packers, dog mushers, camel caravan drivers, builders, carpenters, electricians, plumbers, shoe tiers, college professors (like me), friends, foes, anglers, cavers, hunters, trappers, cast net throwers, weavers, quilters, politicians (well, maybe not politicians), knitters, jewelry makers, linemen, voyagers, yurt builders, dog walkers, rope course instructors, canopy tour guides, … You get the point—anyone that handled cordage. All of these folks tied knots and learned or developed tricks to their trade. Many of these tricks were then passed from person to person, some possibly for hundreds if not thousands of years.

About the Author

Clyde Carter is associate professor of Wilderness Leadership and Experiential Education at Brevard College in North Carolina. He serves as Adventure Director at Rockbrook Camp in the summers. He has over 35 years experience instructing and directing adventure-based programs in Alaska, Colorado, Minnesota, and the Carolinas. During this time he collected the wide variety of tricks found in this book.

Have a rope in your hand as you go through this book. It's designed to be a hands-on book. Some of the tricks you will pick up right away. Others will require practice.

Most of the tricks in this book can be tied using a three or four foot length of flexible rope. I have found the best rope is woven or braided nylon (or synthetic) rope. You can find this kind of rope sold by the foot or in pre-cut hanks at most building supply, hardware, or marine supply stores. Stay away from the poly-blends. They tend to be too stiff. Look for the most flexible rope you can find. Good diameters are 1/8 inch up to 3/8 inch. Use an electric rope cutter that melts the ends as you cut through the rope, or make sure to melt the ends with a lighter or candle to prevent fraying.

The book is divided into two sections. Section one will focus on tricks for tying practical knots. Over time, practitioners have learned to tie knots more efficiently (which usually means more quickly), and I will share some of those methods for tying basic knots with you. For anyone who uses rope in their work or recreational pursuits, I hope you can pick up some practical tricks to employ. If these knots are unfamiliar, I hope you'll take the time to learn them. It's satisfying when you tie the right knot for the right situation—and even more satisfying when you use a trick to tie it more quickly or efficiently. You can impress your friends (and possibly yourself) if you quickly execute the knot called for.

The second section consists of tricks just for fun. If you are not a knot tier, you may want to start with this section. People in any profession look for ways to make their job more fun. The same goes for those who work with rope. Over time, rope handlers have developed tricks with rope just for entertainment. Many of these tricks come from the world of magic. It is very likely that rope and knot tricks are one of the early forms of magic. Even today, contemporary magicians often have elaborate rope routines and have developed a whole class of magic from working with rope. If you find a real interest in this sort of trick, you may want to continue your study with the work of James Stewart in *Abbott's Encyclopedia of Rope Tricks for Magicians*.

I hope you enjoy!

Warnings and Safety Tips

There are some risks of harm or injury that come with the practice of these knots and tricks. Follow these basic safety guidelines to help manage these risks:

1. Establish a five or six foot safety zone for tricks that require swinging ropes. A swinging rope can leave a good welt or possibly take out an eye. Keep everyone at a safe distance!

2. Children working with rope should always be supervised by an adult.

3. Ropes should never be placed around anyone's neck. Serious injury or death can result.

4. Seek proper instruction from a professional before using any knots in this book in a situation that puts you or anyone else at risk of harm or injury. A knot can lose its integrity by simply pulling it tight incorrectly. It takes a trained eye to see if a knot is tied properly.

5. The tricks in this book are from many areas of interests. Do not use this book as a knot book for specific activities (ie. climbing or mountaineering). Many of these knots and tricks have no place on the side of the mountain.

6. Read #4 above one more time.

Before you get started, review a few basic terms. These terms will be useful in interpreting the instructions.

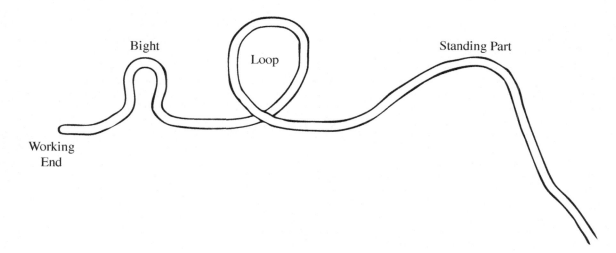

Technically, knots can be divided into three categories: knots, hitches, and bends. Knots form a loop in a rope or a make a knob, hitches secure a rope to another object, and bends tie two ends of ropes together. For the purpose of this book, common names will be used which often confuse these terms. For example, the square knot is technically a bend but is commonly called a knot.

8

Section I:

Tricks For Tying Practical Knots

Overhand Knot

The Overhand is the most basic of knots. It has several practical uses, the most common of which is as a stopper knot. Stopper knots prevent a rope from passing through a hole. This could be a hole in a board (for making a swing or rope ladder), or it could be the hole of a pulley, or even a hole in cloth as used by someone sewing. There are larger stopper knots, but the Overhand is the most basic one. Mountaineers and rock climbers use stopper knots to prevent themselves from rappelling off the ends of their ropes. The most common knot for this is a Double Overhand Knot. An Overhand Knot could also serve as a temporary fix for a fraying rope end.

Of course, to tie this knot you simply make a loop and pass the working end through the loop. The methods for tying Overhands presented in the next few pages offer tricks to tying what might be considered a boring knot.

Whip A Knot

This is the first rope trick I remember learning. A friend at summer camp taught me when I was just 10 years old. When I first saw it, I couldn't believe my eyes. Then when I learned how to do the trick, I remember thinking how easy it was to learn. With a little practice, you will be able to tie an overhand knot in a fraction of a second.

1. Lay the rope across your hand as shown.

3. Hold tight with your index and middle fingers and shake your hand, causing the loop of rope around your hand to fall off.

2. Bring the tips of you fingers up towards your face, then down to pick up the end of the rope on your thumb side. Notice a loop has formed around your hand as you reach for the end. Grab the end of the rope with your index and middle fingers.

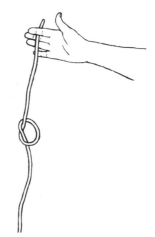

4. An Overhand Knot should form. If not, make sure that you are bringing your fingertips up toward your face before you go down to grab the end.

Follow the diagrams step by step, slowly at first. As you perfect the trick, you can speed up the process and actually *whip* the knot into the rope. Make sure people are keeping a safe distance away as you whip the rope.

Pop A Knot

This trick will take a bit of practice to master, but it's well worth it. Focus on the steps below, not on how the knot is being tied. The knot will just happen. If you try to make it happen, it usually makes things worse.

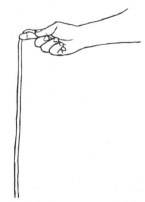

1. Make sure the rope is draped over your finger exactly as in the diagram. Notice that the rope drapes over the end of the finger.

3. Follow through with a downward stroke. As you do, the end will fly through a loop formed above your hand. Don't try to make a loop; it will just happen as you continue to move your hand down. Also, do not attempt to hook your finger around to make a knot. Your arm, hand, and finger will make one straight, fluid movement toward the ground. Don't think about what is happening, just focus on striking the rope about a foot above the end. Like I mentioned, the knot will just form.

2. In a quick motion, bring your hand up a few inches and then immediately down. As you come down, strike the rope downward about one foot up from the end.

Once you perfect this trick, you don't have to start with the rope draped over the end of your finger. Start by holding the rope with all fingers drawn in as shown in the last drawing. As you start the upward movement of the hand, bring your index finger out and then continue with your downward strike. This makes the trick look more natural.

Roll A Knot

Here is another trick that takes practice but is impressive once you have mastered it.

1. Hold the rope as shown in the diagram.

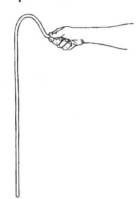

2. Quickly bring your hand up causing a bight to form above your hand.

3. Immediately swing your hand in a circular motion, causing the standing end from your hand to hit the back of the working end. Your hand never hits the rope; the rope hits itself.

4. The loop will roll down the rope and up under the end to form the knot.

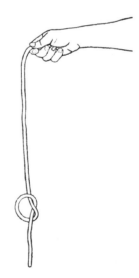

The knot usually forms near the end of the rope. In this case you can roll a second knot farther up the rope—possibly even a third. I find that once you get a good knot set at the end of the rope, the second and third knots are easier to roll. You are getting really good if you can get a fourth and fifth!

Roll A Knot With Weighted Rope

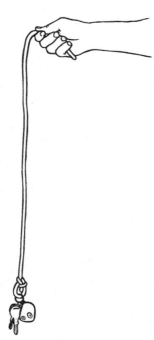

3. Allow the loop of rope to swing down under the weighted object.

1. For this trick you will need to tie a weighted object like a set of keys onto the end of the rope, or you could even tie a large knot such as a Monkey's Fist.

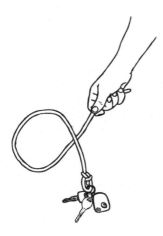

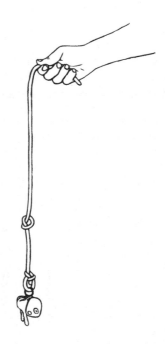

2. In a quick motion, bring your hand up about one or two feet and then immediately swing a loop into the rope.

4. As the weighted object drops back down through the loop, the knot forms. I have seen this trick done with a ten-foot rope while standing on a ladder.

Flip A Knot

Here's another clever way to tie an Overhand.

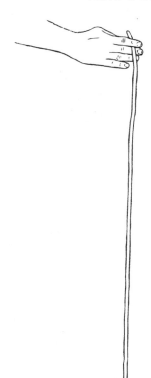

3. As the rope comes over your fingers, hit the center of the rope, causing the end to go through the loop created under your hand.

1. Hold the rope as shown.

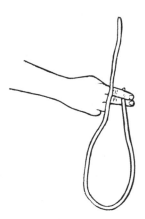

2. Slowly swing the rope until the end can be swung straight out away from you, causing the end to go above your fingers.

4. Drop the loop off your hand before the end has time to swing back out.

Drop A Knot

1. This trick is very similar to flipping a knot. The only difference is that you start with the rope in a horizontal position.

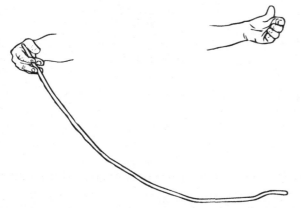

2. Release the end of the rope from your left hand.

3. As the rope swings up and back over the top of your right hand, hit it with your fingers.

4. This will cause the end to pass through the loop under your hand.

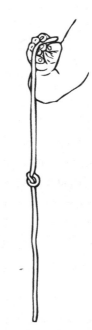

5. Make sure to drop the loop off your hand before the free end swings back out of the loop.

This takes practice; but once mastered, it appears as if the rope naturally uses gravity to form a knot. Of course, you are subtly guiding the end of the rope with your right hand.

Overhand As A Safety Knot

An Overhand is a great knot for backing up knots that may spill (fall apart). This is a trick for tying an Overhand as a back-up safety knot. The problem with Overhand safety knots is that they're often tied the wrong way or in the wrong direction. Using this method will assure the knot is tied correctly and in the right direction.

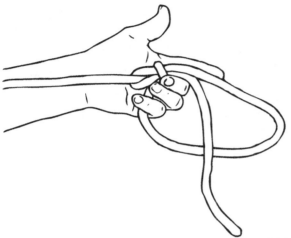

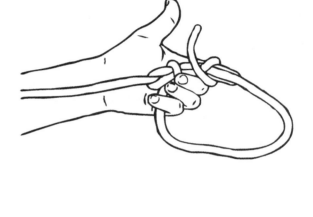

1. Start with the knot you are backing up in your hand with your index finger pointing parallel to the rope you want to tie the Overhand around. This example is with a Bowline. The safety knot for a Bowline should be tied to the standing part coming out of the bight.

2. Wrap the working end of the rope around your finger and the rope next to it. It will make a complete loop.

3. Then remove your finger and insert the working end where your finger was. When tying a safety knot, it should be up close to the knot it is backing up.

Double Overhand As A Safety Knot

What's better than a safety knot? A double safety knot! This is a trick to assure tying the double overhand safety correctly and in the right direction every time. This example is with a Figure Eight on a Bight.

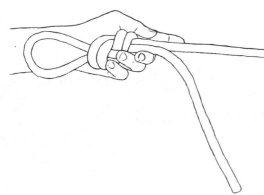

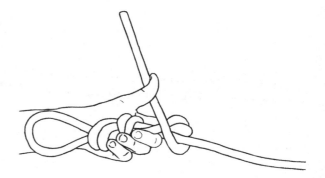

1. Start with the knot you're backing up in your hand with your index finger pointing parallel to the rope you want to tie the Overhand around. The safety knot for a Figure Eight on a Bight should be tied to the standing part coming out of the knot.

2. Wrap the working end around your finger and the rope next to it.

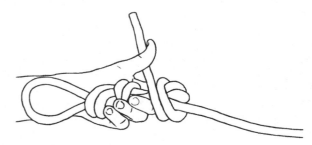

3. Then make a second wrap. Notice you are wrapping back toward the Figure Eight, not away from it.

4. Then remove your finger, and insert the working end where your finger was.

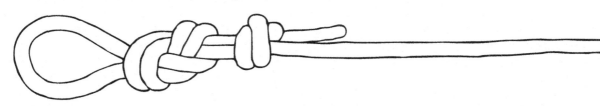

Slip Knot

The Slip Knot (also called an Overhand Noose) forms a loop in the rope that can be adjusted by slipping the rope through the knot.

Whip A Slip

This trick is much like the Overhand Whip-a-Knot. It looks difficult, but it's easy to perform. With a little practice you can tie a Slip Knot in a fraction of a second!

1. Lay the rope across your hand as shown. Notice that the end coming down from your thumb is longer than the other end.

3. As you go down, pick up the long end of the rope about twelve inches above the end with your index and middle fingers.

2. Bring the tips of you fingers up towards your face before going down to pick up the long end.

4. Hold tight with your index and middle fingers and whip your hand, causing the loop of rope around your hand to fall off. A Slip Knot should form.

Follow the diagrams step by step, slowly at first. As you perfect the trick you can speed up the process and actually whip the knot into the rope. Make sure people are a safe distance away as you whip the rope!

With practice, you can eventually take a rope in each hand and tie two knots at the same time—even two different kinds of knots: the Overhand in one hand and the Slip Knot in the other!

Figure Eight Knot

The Figure Eight Knot is a stopper knot that is a bit larger than the Overhand and easier to untie. There are many knots tied using the figure eight configuration that make up the Figure Eight Knot family. Figure Eight Knots include: Figure Eight on a Bight, Figure Eight Follow-Through, Directional Eight, the Flemish Bend, and more. Figure Eight Knots are commonly used in mountaineering and climbing because of their reliability and ease of untying. To tie a Figure Eight, start with a loop in the rope, then add a half turn in the loop and pass the working end through the loop. Of course, there are many fun ways to tie the knot as well...

Twist An Eight

This trick takes a little practice to master.

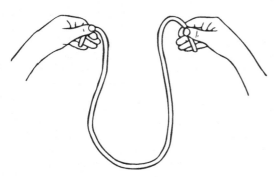

1. Hold the ends of the rope with both hands.

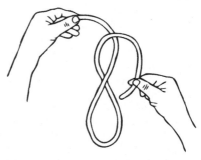

4. Before the loop untwists, throw the end of the rope in your right hand through the loop.

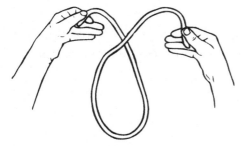

2. Swing your right hand in toward you causing a full loop to form in the rope.

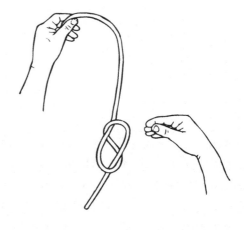

3. Allow the loop to continue to twist another half turn.

As you work on this one, it helps to practice twisting the loop several times before attempting to throw the end through. This allows you to see your target for the throw before attempting it. It's easy to not twist enough or to twist too much. Not twisting enough will produce an Overhand Knot. Twisting too much will produce a knot called the Stevedore.

Roll An Eight

This trick is difficult and takes practice! I have seen several methods to roll an eight. The only method I have mastered is as follows:

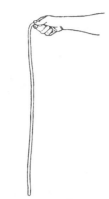

1. Hold the rope as shown.

2. Start with a slight upward movement of your hand followed by an immediate twist with your hand forming a loop of rope that works its way to the end. Notice the thumb should twist down.

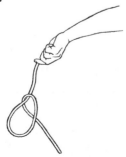

3. Continue the roll of the rope by rolling your hand all the way upside down.

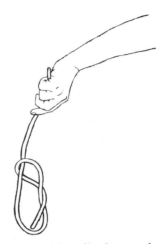

4. The end should roll through the loop forming a Figure Eight Knot.

This is not an easy trick and takes lots of practice. Good luck!

Whip An Eight

This trick is very similar to whipping an Overhand Knot and a Slip Knot, but just a bit more complicated. It would be best to master whipping an Overhand Knot and a Slip Knot before working on this one.

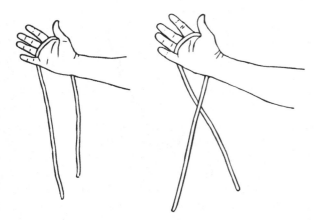

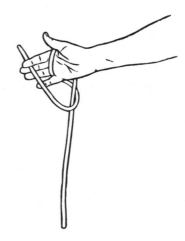

1. Lay the rope across your hand as shown. Move your hand in a circular motion, causing the end coming down from your little finger to swing around the end coming down from your thumb.

3. As you go down, pick up the end of the rope with your index and middle fingers.

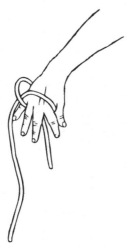

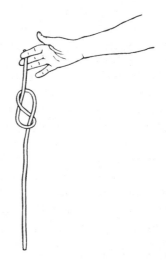

2. As the end swings around, bring the tips of your fingers up toward your face and then down to pick up the end of the rope coming down from your little finger.

4. Hold tight with your index and middle fingers while you whip your hand, causing the loop of rope around your hand to fall off. A Figure Eight Knot should form.

Quick Figure Eight

For some reason new knot tiers often have a difficult time tying the Figure Eight consistently. There are many tricks to correct this. Here's how I teach new knot tiers how to tie the eight; it happens to be a quick way to do it as well.

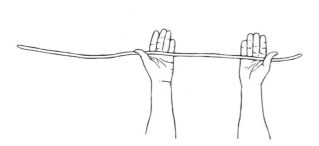

1. First, lay the rope across both hands.

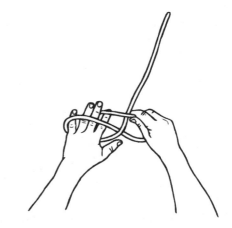

3. With your right hand, pass the end over the standing part and into the fingers of your left hand.

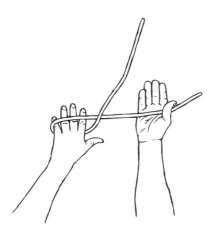

2. Flip your left hand over, causing the standing end to fall between your hands. The rope will form a loop around your left hand.

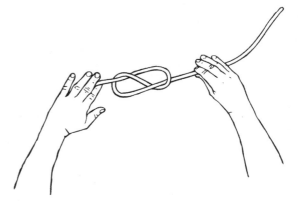

4. Remove your left hand from the loop, taking the working end with it.

Quick Figure Eight On A Bight

The Figure Eight on a bight can also be tied with the exact same method. The only difference is that you hold a large bight in your hand instead of a single strand of rope. This will require a longer rope—maybe six feet or longer. The end result is a loop in the end of your rope that does not slip. Of course it is also a quick loop in the end of the rope that does not slip.

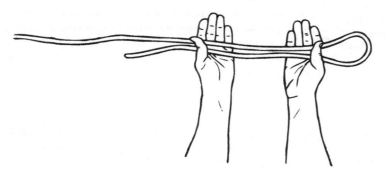

1. Form a large bight with the end of the rope and drape it over both hands as shown.

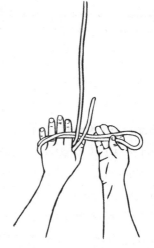

2. Flip your left hand over, causing the standing ends to fall between your hands. The ropes will form a loop around your left hand.

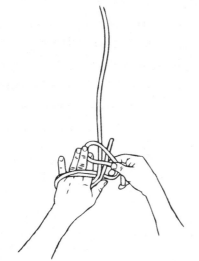

3. Place the bight between the index and middle fingers of your left hand.

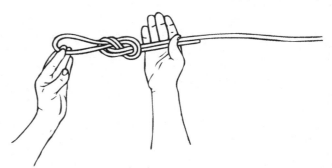

4. Pull the bight through the loop on your left hand. With practice you can tie this knot in less than one second!

Square Knot

 The Square Knot (also known as the Reef Knot) is used to tie two ends of rope of equal diameters together. Tied properly, it should not slip. Whenever you need to tie two ropes together temporarily, this knot is a good choice. However, it's not recommended for supporting life (i.e. any form of climbing) because it can easily lose integrity when pulled incorrectly. To tie a Square Knot, start with one end of rope in each hand. Place the rope in your right hand over the left end and wrap it around the left rope. Then take the rope that is now in your left hand and place it over the right end. Wrap it around the right rope to form a bight on a bight. The saying goes "right over left, left over right, makes a bight on a bight." The most common mistake is to instead tie a Granny Knot - right over left, right over left. The Granny Knot will not hold under pressure.

One Second Square Knot

This trick requires two ropes; each should be at least four feet long. The more flexible the ropes are, the better.

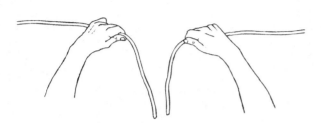

1. Hold the ropes as shown with at least eight inches of rope dangling from each hand.

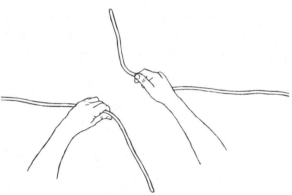

2. Cause the rope in your right hand to sway by slowly rocking it away and then towards your left hand.

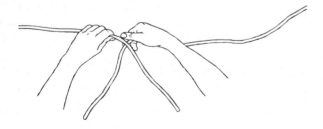

3. In a quick motion, hit the left end with the right hand causing the right end to flip all around the left end.

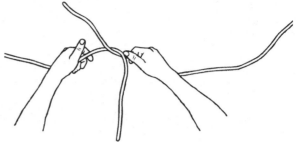

4. As this happens, the left end will fly up.

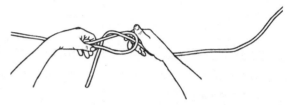

5. Catch it with the left hand, creating a bight. The right end will continue to whip around the bight. It's important to keep the right end's momentum going.

6. As the right end comes around the second time, catch it with the thumb and fingers of the right hand.

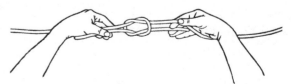

7. Pull the end through the bight that just formed on the right hand.

Untying The Square Knot

When a Square Knot has been pulled tight, you can use this method to easily untie it.

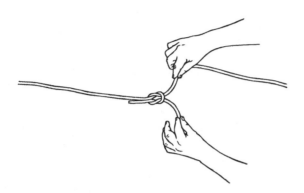

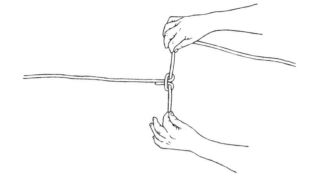

1. From one side of the knot, take the standing end in one hand and the working end in the other.

2. Pull hard and quickly, causing the knot to "pop" into what is commonly called a Lark's Head. This is a knot that slips.

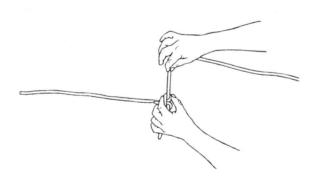

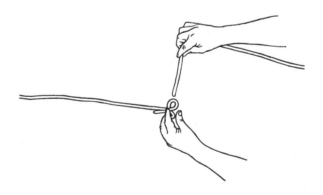

Hold the knot in one hand as you pull the standing end to slide the knot off the end of the rope.

This is why the Square Knot should not be used for supporting life. If it is accidently pulled into a Lark's Head, it can fall apart. This is, however, a convenient way to untie the knot.

Bowline

The Bowline forms a loop at the end of a rope that does not slip. It's important to know that this knot can be tied correctly yet still lose its form when tightened down. If this happens, the knot can fall apart. To recognize a correctly tied Bowline, look for a bight tied around a loop (see picture above). This is a great knot to use when you need to secure a rope around an object, particularly if you do not want the knot to slip up tight against the object. To tie a Bowline, you can put a loop in the standing part of the rope with the standing end on the bottom. Pass the working end up through the loop, around the standing end, and back through the loop.

One Handed Bowline

This is a method for tying a Bowline around your waist with one hand. You will need more than six feet of flexible rope for this trick. When tied properly, the Bowline creates a loop that does not slip. Who knows—perhaps this could save a life in an emergency situation.

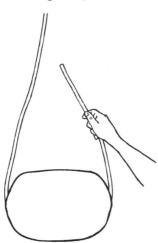

1. Wrap the rope around your waist so that the working end is in your right hand and the standing part is in your left hand. Left-handed people can reverse the whole process. Notice that you have about ten inches of the working end of the rope beyond your hand.

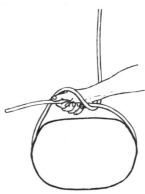

3. Turn your right hand down, causing the free end to pass under the standing part. Next you do a move that I call, "scratching your belly." As you do this, allow a bit of slack in the standing part and keep a firm hand on the working end. Bring the standing end up your belly and then turn your palm up.

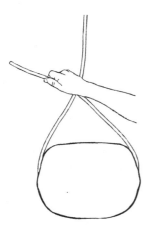

2. Cross your entire right hand over the top of the standing part.

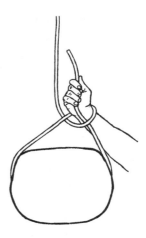

4. Now you should have a loop of rope with the standing part and your right arm through the loop holding onto the working end.

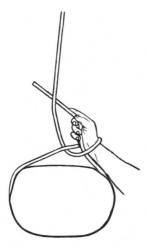

5. Pass the working end around the standing part and let go to grab it on the other side.

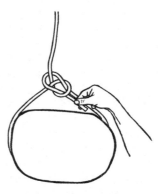

7. Pull the knot tight against the standing part. You should have a loop in the standing part and a bight in the working end—the Bowline.

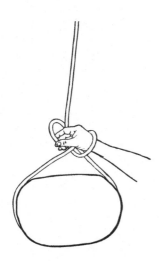

6. Pull the working end back through the loop on the standing part as you pull your right hand out.

8. A Bowline should never be considered complete without a backup Overhand Knot securing the bight. As mentioned, this knot can easily fall apart if it is pulled the wrong direction. That's why it's important to make sure you see the loop and bight, and that you back it up with an Overhand Knot.

The One-Handed Bowline can be tied quickly with some practice. Your left hand is not needed in the process if the standing part of the rope is long enough or secured to some object. However, it helps to practice with your left hand loosely holding onto the standing part.

Bowline From A Slip Knot

1. Tie a loose Slip Knot in the standing part of the rope. Of course, this could be done quickly with one hand using the Quick Slip Knot trick on page 19. It is important to keep this knot loose.

4. When the knot is snug, hold the Overhand firmly and continue to pull until the knot "pops" into a Bowline.

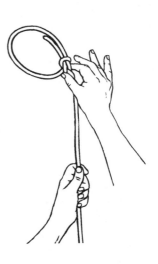

2. Place the end that does not slip through the bight, on top of the Overhand.

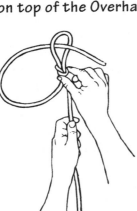

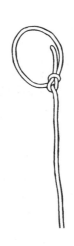

3. Hold onto the Overhand Knot with one hand, and pull the standing part with the other.

Bowline From A Flip

This is another great method for tying a Bowline if you ever need a quick loop in the end of the rope.

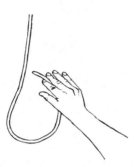

1. Hold the rope as shown between your index finger and middle finger.

2. Grab the standing part of the rope with your thumb under the standing part and fingers on top.

3. Now for the tricky part: fold your hand under and up through the loop of rope you have formed. This is done without letting go of the either part of the rope. It may take a bit of practice to master.

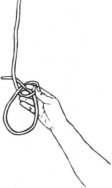

4. Use your other hand to take the working end around the standing part.

5. Place the working end back in the fingers of your right hand and pull it through the loop.

With a bit of practice, you can do this using only one hand!

Quick Bowline To A Post

1. Wrap the rope around the post with the working end coming around the left side of the post.

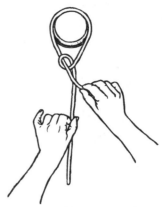

3. Hold the standing part loosely while pulling firmly on the working end. The working end will be straight with the standing part forming a loop around it.

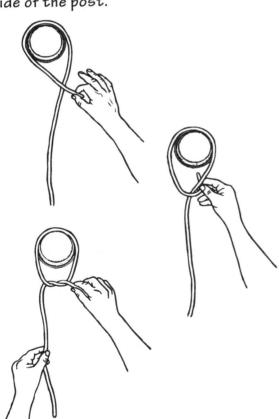

2. Cross the working end over, then under the standing part creating an Overhand Knot around the post.

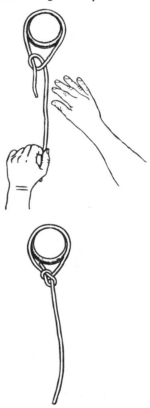

4. Wrap the working end around the standing part and passing it back through the loop on the standing part.

One characteristic that makes a knot useful is that it can be easily untied. When a Bowline has been pulled tight, you can use this method to untie it easily. It's called "breaking the back" of a Bowline.

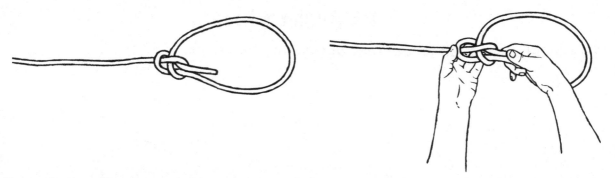

Turn the bowline over and bend the bight back as if you are "breaking the back" of the Bowline.

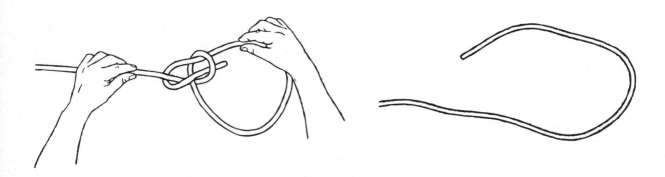

This loosens up the knot so it is easily untied.

Angler's Loop

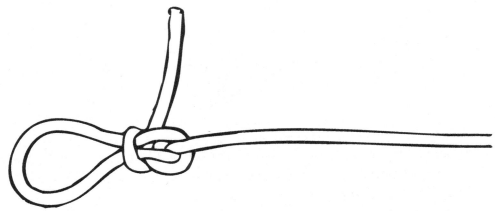

The Angler's Loop also forms a loop at the end of rope that does not slip. However, the Quick Angler's Loop only produces a small loop.

Quick Angler's Loop

You should have at least four feet of rope for this trick.

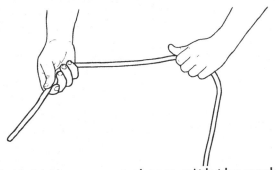

1. Hold the rope as shown, with the working end hanging about ten to twelve inches past the right hand.

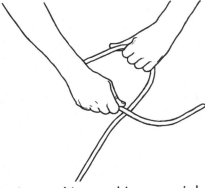

2. Flip the working end in your right hand over the standing part below your left hand, causing a bight of rope to form in your left hand.

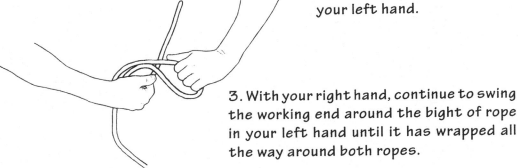

3. With your right hand, continue to swing the working end around the bight of rope in your left hand until it has wrapped all the way around both ropes.

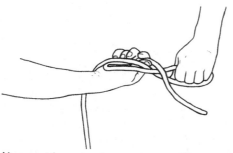

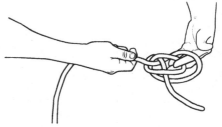

4. Keep the momentum going, allowing the working end to land over the rope between your hands.

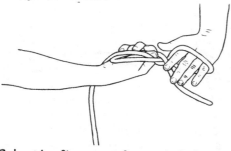

5. Poke the fingers of your left hand down through the bight while lifting them over the working end of the rope.

6. Pick up the bight on your right thumb with the index and middle fingers of your left hand.

7. Pull that bight through the bight on your left hand while holding only the standing part with your right hand.

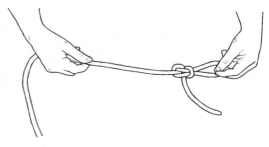

8. As you pull this bight through, the Angler's Knot will form on the end of the rope.

Girth Hitching The Angler's Loop

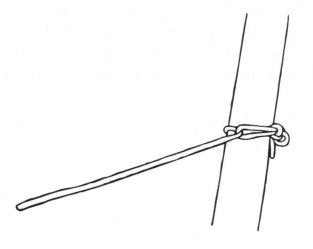

To attach the rope quickly to a tree or post, tie a Quick Angler's Loop on the end of the rope. Pass the knot around the tree or post, and pull the standing end through the loop to form a Girth Hitch. This can also be done with a Bowline or Figure Eight on a Bight. Girth Hitches are not recommended for supporting life, i.e. any form of climbing.

Clove Hitch

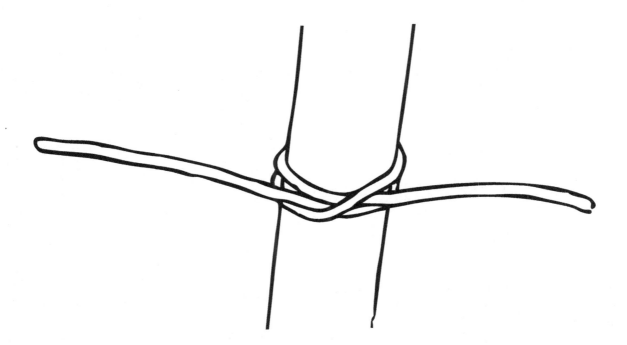

The Clove Hitch constricts around the object it is tied to. It makes a great temporary attachment. Boaters use it to tie off boats, and climbers use it to attach to anchors. It can also serve as an attachment when lashing logs or poles together. It is an especially handy way to attach things because you can change its position along the rope without untying it by simply working the rope through the hitch.

Picking Up A Clove Hitch

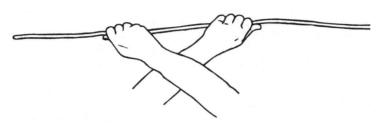

1. Start with the rope lying on the ground or a table. Pick up the rope as shown with your hands crossed.

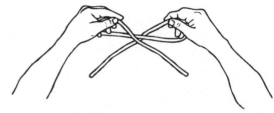

2. Pull your hands past each other without twisting or flipping them. The rope should form two loops.

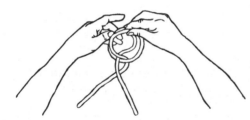

3. Place the loop in your right hand on top of the loop in your left. Make sure not to flip or fold this loop over, just place it on top of the other loop.

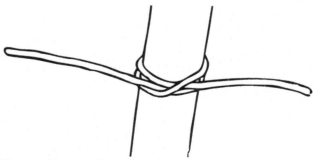

4. Place the two loops onto the object where you would like the Clove Hitch and pull the ends snug.

1. Hold the rope as shown.

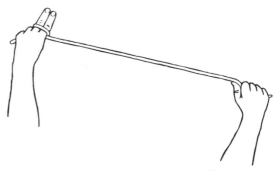

4. Pull the loop high onto the fingers using the rope in your right hand.

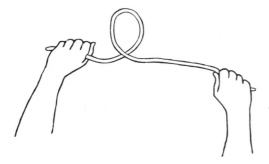

2. Use your right hand to throw an overhand loop. It is best to do this on a table or on the ground. In time you can do this in the air, making the trick much more impressive.

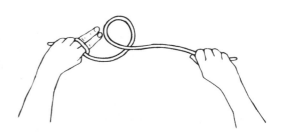

5. Throw a second overhand loop and pull it up in the same manner.

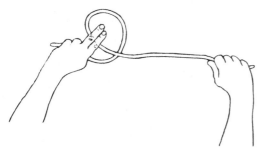

3. Place your index and middle fingers in the loop on the table (or in the air).

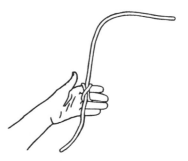

6. Now you have a Clove Hitch on your fingers. Place the two loops onto the object where you would like the Clove Hitch.

This quick method is for tying a Clove Hitch around a tree or post. You will need at least six feet of rope for this trick. You can use this method on a vertical or horizontal post. Start with about three feet of working end hanging from your hand.

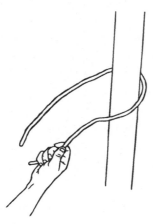

1. Throw the working end around the post with enough momentum to wrap around the post twice.

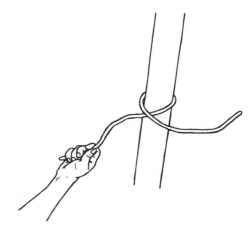

2. You will have to aim as you throw to cause the rope to form an "X" on the first pass.

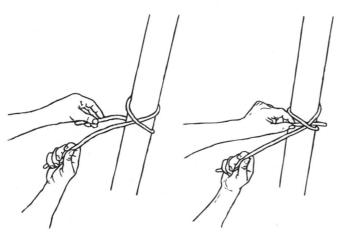

3. As the rope comes around the second time grab the end with your left hand and slide it under the "X" formed on the post.

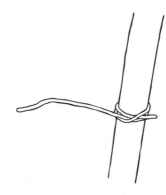

It may be easier to pick up the "X" with your right hand and as you pass the working end under.

One Hand Clove Hitch

With practice, this can be performed in one fluid motion, creating a Clove Hitch in a matter of seconds.

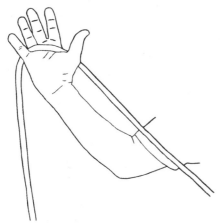

1. Start with the rope draped across the palm and resting in the thumb and little finger as shown.

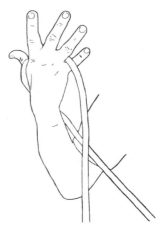

2. Turn your palm inward, creating a loop.

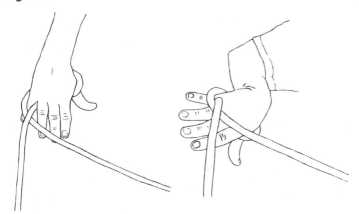

3. Swing your fingertips down and outward.

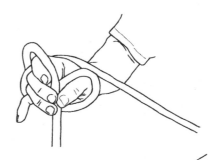

4. Grab the farthest rope from you, allowing the two loops to slide onto your thumb.

Make sure to test the hitch!
One wrong twist and you don't have a Clove Hitch.

One Hand Clove Hitch Clip

This is a method to clip a Clove Hitch onto a carabiner with one hand. Seek professional training before using this hitch to support life.

1. First clip the rope into the carabiner.

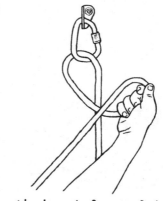

4. Cross the loop in front of the carabiner.

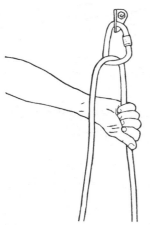

2. With your right hand, grab the rope coming out of the back of the carabiner, with your thumb pointing down.

5. Clip the loop into the carabiner.

3. Point your thumb up as you pull the rope from behind the carabiner.

Make sure to test the hitch. One wrong twist and you do not have a Clove Hitch.

Munter Hitch

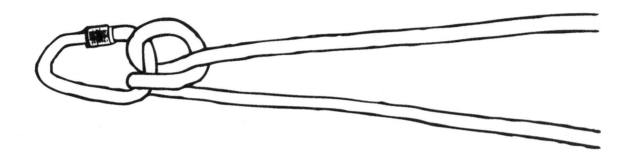

The Munter Hitch is a friction hitch used in mountaineering as a belay. Seek professional training before using it to support life.

One Hand Munter Hitch

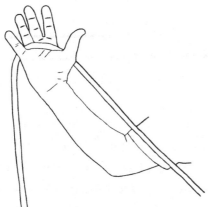

1. Start with the rope draped across the palm, resting in the thumb and little finger as shown.

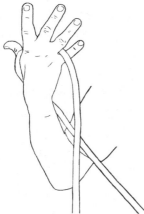

2. Turn your palm inward, creating a loop.

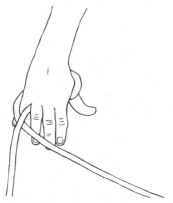

3. Swing your fingers down and outward.

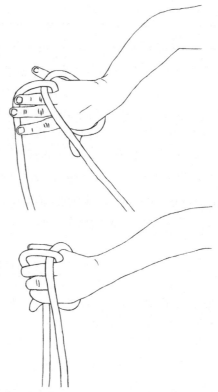

4. grab the far rope exactly as shown.

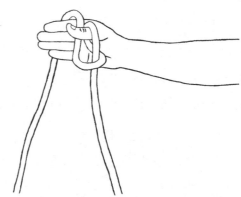

5. Slide the hitch onto your thumb.

This trick is similar to the One Hand Clove Hitch, except for how you grab onto the far rope. For the Munter Hitch, you grab it from the inside; for the Clove Hitch, you grab it from the outside.

Fisherman's Knot

The Fisherman's Knot is great for tying two pieces of rope together. Once you pull this knot tight, it will be difficult to untie. This is one of several knots that have been referred to over time as the "True Love Knot" or "Friendship Knot." This knot is formed by tying an Overhand Knot in the working end of each rope around the standing part of the other rope. Then the two Overhand Knots are pulled together.

Quick Fisherman's Knot

This is the *Quick* Fisherman's Knot because both Overhand Knots are tied around the opposing standing parts at the same time.

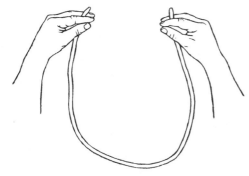

1. Hold the ends of the rope as shown.

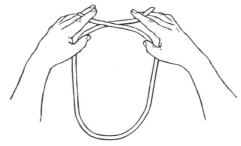

3. Now with your left thumb, reach behind and hook the right rope. Pull the ropes apart to form the shape of an "X."

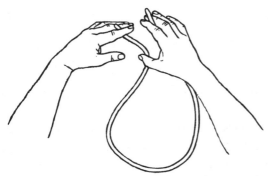

2. With your right thumb, hook the rope on the left.

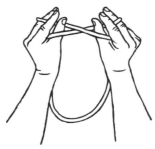

4. Poke your thumbs up through the 'X' as shown.

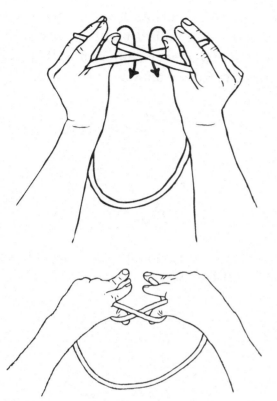

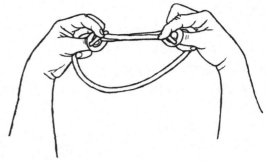

7. Now pull your thumbs out of the loops taking the ends of each rope as you go. This will require some assistance from the fingers holding the ends.

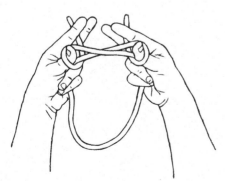

5. Move your thumbs in the pattern following the arrows, making sure to hook each working end as you go.

8. Pull the standing parts tight.

The Overhands will slide together to complete the Fisherman's Knot.

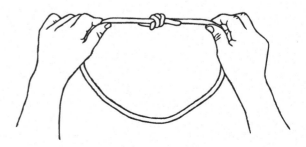

6. You should have a loop of rope around each thumb as shown.

Quick True Fisherman's Knot

For those who really know their knots, the Quick Fisherman's Knot on the previous pages is not a "true" Fisherman's Knot. The two Overhand Knots are opposite to each other and don't fit nicely together when pulled tight. In order for the knots to fit nicely together, they must be tied to mirror each other. It's a bit more difficult, but to get a true Fisherman's Knot, follow these directions:

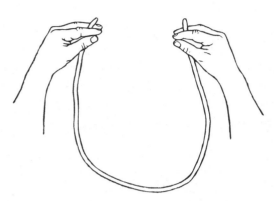

1. Hold the ends of the rope as shown.

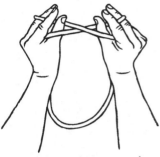

4. Place your thumbs up through the sides of the 'X.'

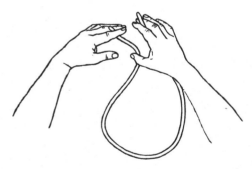

2. Hook each rope with the opposite thumb.

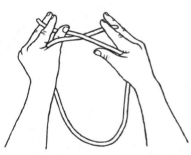

5. The next steps are a bit tricky, so take a close look at the pictures. Take your right thumb out of the 'X.'

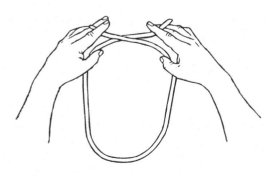

3. This forms an 'X.'

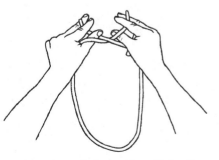

6. While maintaining the 'X,' place your thumb through from the top, and hook the rope with your right thumb.

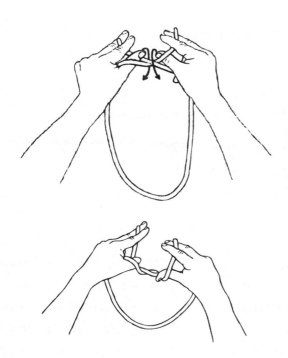

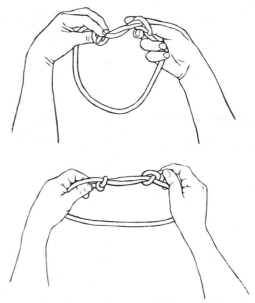

7. Move your thumbs in the pattern following the arrows, making sure to hook the working ends as you go. Notice that the left thumb moves away from you in a circular motion while the right thumb moves towards you in a circular motion.

9. Now pull your thumbs out of the loops, pulling the ends of the rope with them. This will require some assistance from the fingers to hold the ends.

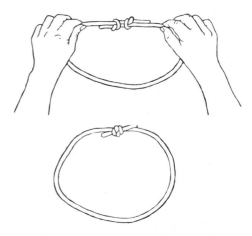

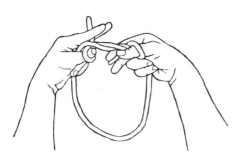

8. You should have a loop of rope around each thumb.

10. Pull tight and you have the true Fisherman's Knot.

This method requires a bit more practice than the previous method.

Double Fisherman's Knot

The Double Fisherman's Knot is similar to the Fisherman's, except that you use Double Overhand Knots when tying it. This knot is commonly used in mountaineering and climbing to make Prusik loops—where the two ends of a small-diameter rope are tied together. This knot is a good choice when the ropes need to be tied together permanently. Once this knot is tightened, it is difficult to untie.

Quick True Fisherman's Knot

The Double Fisherman's Knot can be tied in the same fashion as the Quick Fisherman's Knot. As with the Fisherman's Knot, the two Double Overhand Knots must mirror each other to be a true Double Fisherman's Knot. The following directions show how to tie the quick "true" Double Fisherman's Knot.

Follow the directions for the Quick True Fisherman's Knot (page 48) up to step 8.

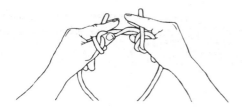

9. Then hook your thumbs around once more.

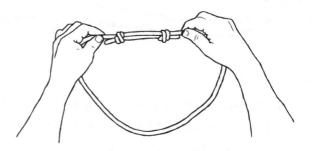

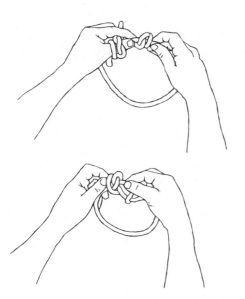

11. Once you have the ends through the loops, you may have to 'dress' the knots before you pull them together. Notice the pattern of each knot in the drawing. You may have to flip and fold some loops over to form this pattern.

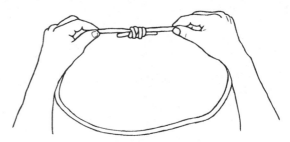

10. Now pull your thumbs out of the loops, pulling the ends of the rope with them. This will require some assistance from the fingers to hold the ends. It's difficult to pull the ends through two loops, so it may be best to pull one through at a time with a little assistance from the fingers of each hand.

12. If the knots are 'dressed' properly, they should fit nicely together once you pull them tight.

Fisherman's Loop

The Fisherman's Loop is not a very common knot, but it's fun to tie. This knot was used in the early years of mountaineering to tie the "middle man" onto a climbing rope. You can tie this knot in the middle of a long rope without using the ends. Other knots replaced this knot in mountaineering long ago. The Fisherman's Loop has also been called the True Love Knot.

Quick Fisherman's Loop

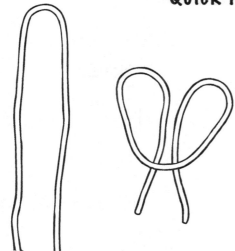

1. Start by taking a large bight in the rope and folding it over on top of itself.

2. Then take the loop formed on the right and overlap the loop on the left.

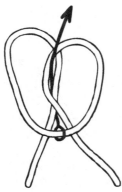

3. Pull the bight under the 'X' and through the hole formed by the overlapping loops as indicated by the arrow.

4. Each standing part should form an Overhand.

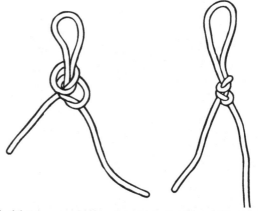

5. You may have to untangle them a bit before pulling them tightly together.

Just like with the Fisherman's Knot, the above method does not tie a "true" Fisherman's Loop because the Overhand Knots do not mirror each other. There are a couple of remedies for this...

Quick True Fisherman's Loop

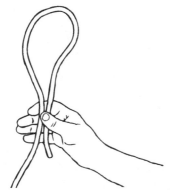

1. Start with a bight in you right hand.

2. Lay the bight on a table, forcing two identical loops to form on each strand of the bight. This move is a bit tricky, but it can become quick and smooth with practice.

3. Take the loop formed on the left side and place it on top of the loop on the right side.

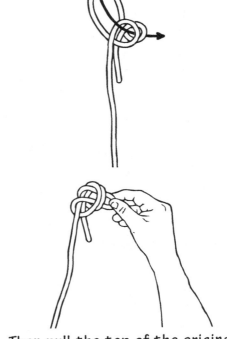

4. Then pull the top of the original bight down through the two loops.

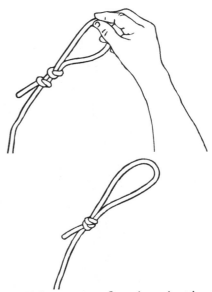

5. This will form two Overhands that may have to be untangled to form the Fisherman's Loop.

Here is another method for tying a true Fisherman's Loop.

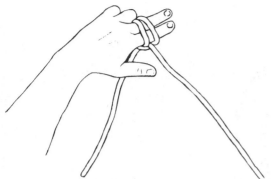

1. Start by throwing a Clove Hitch on your fingers (see page 40). The clove hitch is made up of two loops.

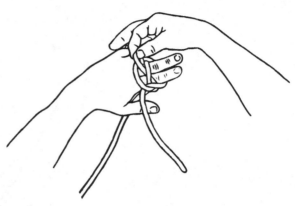

4. Then take the loop that's now on the far right and pull it under the one next to it and out between the two.

2. Now, throw a third loop on your fingers.

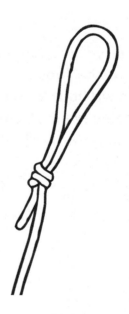

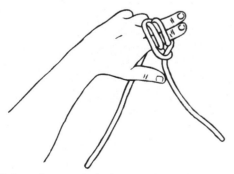

3. Take the new loop over the two that form the Clove Hitch.

5. Take the rope off of your left hand and pull the two Overhands tightly together.

Butterfly Knot

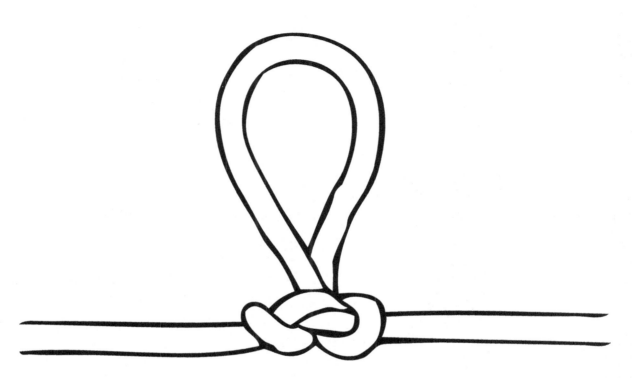

The Butterfly Knot is used to tie a loop in the middle of a rope. The ends come out of the loop in opposite directions, so that tension can be put on the rope without distorting the knot. This knot is used often in rescue and mountaineering. It can also be used to isolate a weak spot in the rope. There are many ways tie it. Let's look at one of the quicker ways...

Quick Butterfly Knot

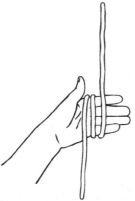

1. Wrap the rope around your left hand three times as shown.

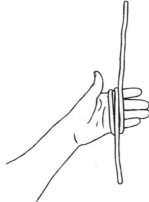

2. Pick up the loop on the far left and lay it between the two other loops.

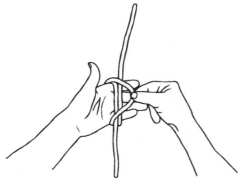

3. Pick up the loop that is now on the far left. Cross it over all loops, and lay it between the Index and ring fingers of your left hand.

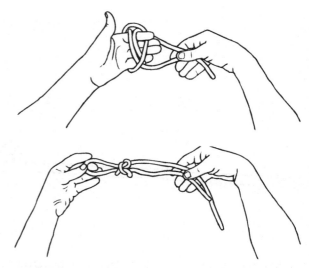

4. Pull the rope through the loops as you remove your hand from the loops.

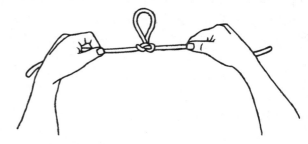

5. Pull the two standing parts to allow the knot to take its shape. Some refer to this step as spreading the butterfly wings. The wings are the two loops you can see on the bottom of the knot once it is pulled into shape.

Sheet Bend

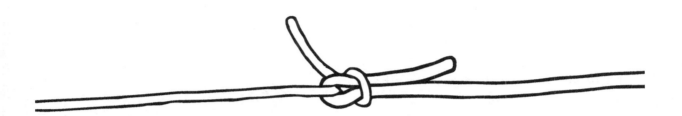

I learned as a young boy in Scouts that this was the knot to use if you ever had to tie bed sheets together to climb out the window of a burning building. I have never had the opportunity to test this, but it made sense to me. However, maybe the knot's name came from the nautical field, where sheets refer to lines (rope, cables). Regardless, this knot works well when you need to tie two ropes of unequal diameters or different materials together. Notice that the knot is a loop on a bight. The bight is generally tied with the thicker or stiffer rope.

1. Tie a *quick Slip Knot* (see page 19) in the thinner diameter rope, and keep it loose.

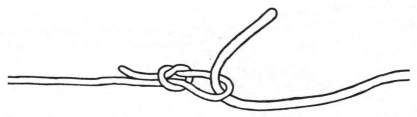

2. Place the end of the larger diameter rope through the bight of the Slip Knot.

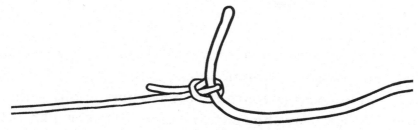

3. Wrap one hand around the overhand of the Slip Knot, and hold tight while you pull the end that slips with the other hand.

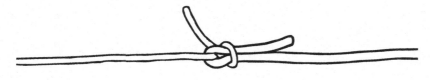

4. When the knot is snug, hold the Overhand firmly and continue to pull until the knot "pops" into a Sheet Bend. You will know that the Sheet Bend has formed when you see a bight form in the larger diameter rope. This knot looks a lot like a Bowline. The smaller diameter rope will form a loop around the bight.

This method of tying the Sheet Bend is also often used to tie two small diameter strings or even thread together. It is easier than tying a Square Knot in small thread.

Trucker's Hitch

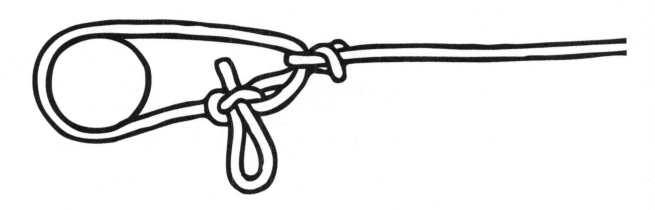

The Trucker's Hitch is used to cinch a rope tight. Truckers use this hitch to secure loads on a trailer. I use it to tie canoes and kayaks to the racks on my car. One end is fixed (secured) to the rack on one side of the boat. The rope is then tossed over the boat and tied with a Trucker's Hitch on the other side.

There are many ways to tie a Trucker's Hitch, but this is the one that I find is quickest to tie and untie. That's why I've chosen to put it in this book. You will need at least six feet of rope. One end should be fixed at a distant point. I generally use a Bowline on the distant point. Another popular knot for the distant point is a Girth Hitched Overhand on a Bight.

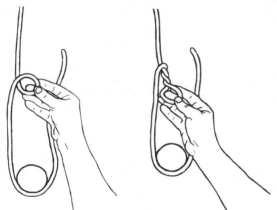

1. Begin by twisting the standing end several times with your right hand.

3. Pass the working end around the object you wish to cinch to and back through the bight of the Slip Knot.

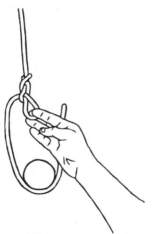

2. Pull a bight of rope from below the twists that you created, and put it through the loop. This makes a Slip Knot. The extra twists make this knot easier to untie. You want to make sure it has more than one twist.

4. Pull snug. This set up gives you a bit of a mechanical advantage, almost 3 to 1. Once tight, hold the pressure by pinching with one hand where the two bights meet while you tie a Half-Hitch around the standing end with your other hand. You can make it a slippery Half-Hitch to make untying the knot easier. Make sure this Half-Hitch is secure. Sometimes I tie a second Half-Hitch with the end instead of the slippery Half-Hitch.

This knot takes practice to be able to maintain the tension as you tie off the Half-Hitches.

Taut Line Hitch

The Taut-line Hitch forms an adjustable loop. It's a great knot for tying up tents and tarps because it can be tightened or loosened after it's tied. This makes it easy to adjust the tent or tarp to allow adequate water runoff.

This method for tying the Taut-line Hitch allows you to easily untie the knot. This is very useful on a cold day when the knot may be frozen and you do not want to take off your gloves to untie it.

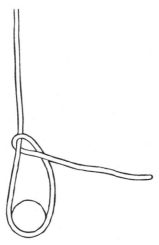

1. Wrap the working end around a tree, post, or stake.

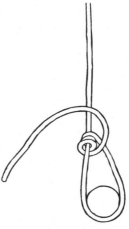

3. Make one final wrap around the standing end on the tent or tarp side.

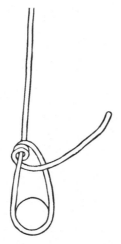

2. Wrap the working end around the standing end three times, working toward the tree or stake.

4. As you tuck the working end under itself, bring a bight through instead of the end. This is the trick that will make it easy to untie the knot.

Many knots can be made "slippery" by pulling a bight through instead of the working end on the last step. Of course, this should not be done on knots in critical positions where you do not want the knot to accidently come untied.

Section II:

Tricks For Fun

I generally make it a habit not to show people the "secrets" to these tricks. Folks have a greater sense of accomplishment if they work it out on their own.

Monkey Chain

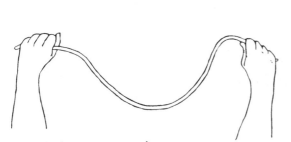

1. Hold the rope as shown.

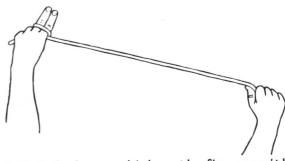

4. Pull the loop up high on the fingers with the rope in your right hand.

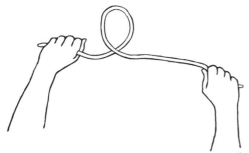

2. Use your right hand to throw an overhand loop. It is best to do this on a table or on the ground. In time you can do this in the air, making the trick much more impressive.

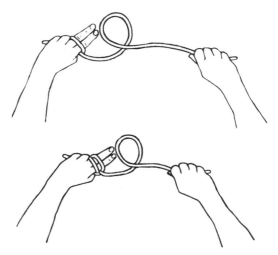

5. Repeat the last two steps several more times, making sure each loop is stacked neatly in front of the loop before it.

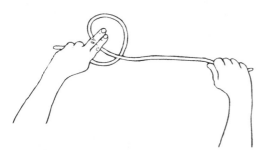

3. Place your index and middle fingers in the loop on the table (or in the air).

6. There should not be any loops crossing others.

7. Place the end of the rope in your right hand between the index and middle fingers on your left hand. Hold tight with these fingers.

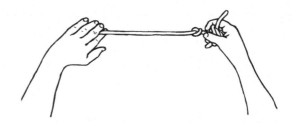

9. Continue pulling the rope with your left hand, making sure to hold all the loops in your right hand.

8. With your right hand, grab all the loops on your left hand and slowly pull the end of the rope through all the loops as you pull the loops off your hand.

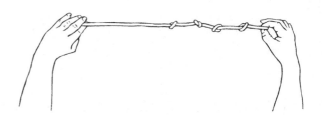

10. Knots will slowly emerge from the stack of loops in your right hand, starting from the bottom of the pile.

I have found this trick entertaining to all ages. When I am showing children ages three to eight, I let the child pull the end of the rope once I get it out through the loop. Their faces light up every time as the knots come pouring out of my hand!

The trick can also be performed with a much larger rope (ten to twenty feet), and instead of throwing loops around your fingers, the rope could be casually looped into larger coils around the left hand. Once you reach the end of the rope, pass the end through the coils and toss the rope while holding onto the end that was passed through the loops.

Three Knot Monkey Chain

This is a bit more complicated than the regular monkey chain and will require a bit of practice. The idea is to do a three-knot monkey chain with each knot being a different knot—a Slip Knot, a Figure Eight Knot, and an Overhand Knot.

1. Hold the rope as shown.

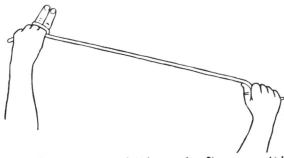

4. Pull the loop up high on the fingers with the rope in your right hand.

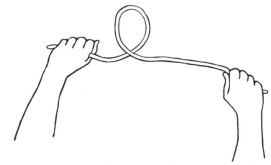

2. Use your right hand to throw an overhand loop. It is best to do this on a table or on the ground. In time you can do this in the air, making the trick much more impressive.

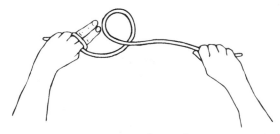

5. Use your right hand to throw a second overhand loop on the table (or in the air).

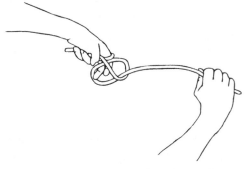

6. This time pick up the loop by going through the back side of the loop with your left hand index and middle fingers. As you pull the loop onto your fingers, you should notice that this loop has an extra twist in it. This will be the Figure Eight Knot when you pull the knots off.

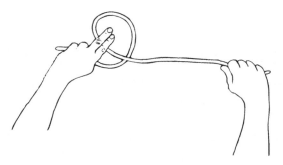

3. Place your index and middle fingers in the loop on the table (or in the air).

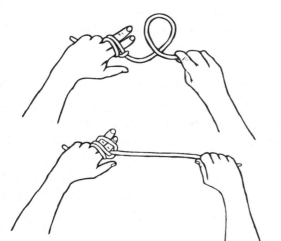

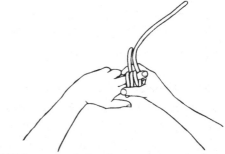

9. With your right hand, hold all the loops on your left hand and slowly pull the end of the rope through all the loops.

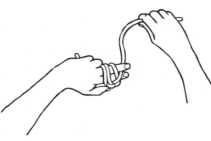

7. Throw another overhand loop and pull it onto your fingers.

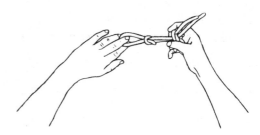

10. Watch carefully as the first knot appears. You want a bight of rope to come through causing a Slip Knot to form.

8. Place the end of the rope from your right hand between the index and middle fingers on your left hand. However, with this monkey chain make sure that about six inches is hanging free. Hold tight with these fingers. If you have too much tail hanging free, the slip knot will extend through the figure eight and possibly the overhand. If you do not have enough tail, the slip knot will pull through into an overhand. With practice you will learn exactly how much tail pull through.

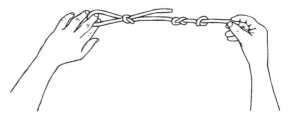

11. The second knot will be your Figure Eight. It will take practice to make sure the bight is not caught up in this knot as well. The third knot will be the Overhand.

It will take some practice to make sure the end of the rope does not pass through the first loop and untie the Slip Knot, or that the end isn't caught up in the Figure Eight Knot.

Don't Let Go

This trick is a classic! I used it in the introduction of this book to make a point about how difficult it is to find the origin of rope tricks. However, this is a version of a trick that appears to have been invented by the late British magician G W Hunter in the early 1900s (James, Tarbell, Fulves).

This trick, above all other tricks, is one that you never ever reveal the secret to. When performed properly it will keep people amazed for days, if not weeks. The only way people should learn the secret is to figure it out on their own! If you want to figure the trick out by yourself, just follow the pictures without reading the text. Good luck.

When introducing "Don't Let Go," state that you are going to take your rope with one end in each hand, and without letting go you are going to tie an Overhand Knot. This may seem simple, but it's actually impossible without knowing the "trick." Demonstrate the trick and then allow others to try. At first, they may randomly try to tie a knot. After a couple of tries, let them follow you step by step. Of course, you don't let them know what you are doing as you roll the rope off your hands.

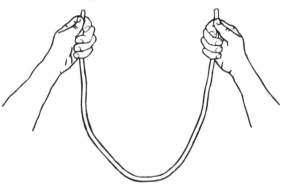

1. Hold the ends of the rope as shown—
ends by the thumbs.

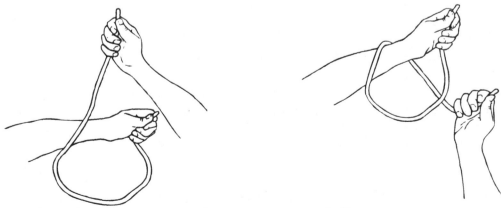

2. Drape the rope over your left arm.

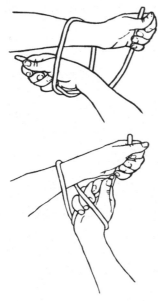

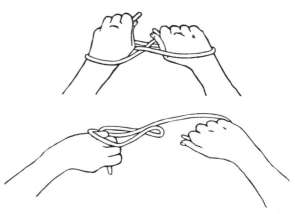

5. Roll the rope off your hands by first turning them down, then pulling them apart.

3. Take the right hand into the hole on the left and out of the hole on the right without letting go of the rope.

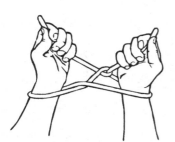

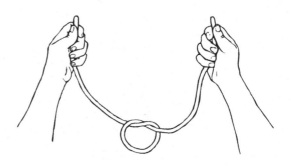

4. Pull snug and your rope should look like the drawing above.

The Trick: It is impossible to tie a knot without letting go of an end. The trick is to let go and grab it again without being seen. This happens as you roll the rope off your hands in the last step. As you turn your hands down, let go with the right hand and immediately grab the end as it passes through the loop next to your hand. As you pull your hands apart, the knot will roll off your left arm.

Don't Let Go—Figure Eight

My good friend John Arnold figured out how to tie a Figure Eight without letting go of the ends. This one is a bit more complicated than the simple Overhand. You should master the Overhand first.

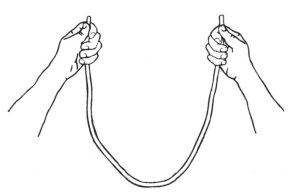

1. Hold the ends of the rope as shown—ends by the thumbs.

3. Pass your right hand through the back of the bight below your arm.

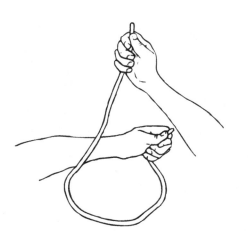

2. Drape the rope over your left arm with your right hand.

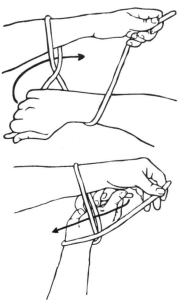

4. Then pass your right hand around to the back and through the loop on your left arm as shown by the arrows.

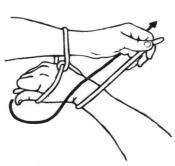

5. Pass your right hand under your left arm as show by the arrow. As you do this you may have to pull the rope coming out of your left hand off your right wrist.

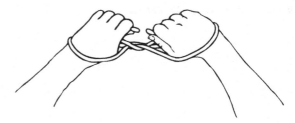

7. Roll the rope off your hands by first turning them down, then pulling them apart.

8. Just as in the Overhand "Don't Let Go," this is where the "trick" is. As you turn your hands down, let go with the right hand and immediately grab the end as it passes through the loop next to your hand.

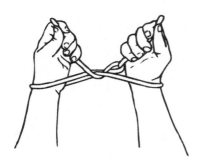

6. Pull snug, and your rope should look like this.

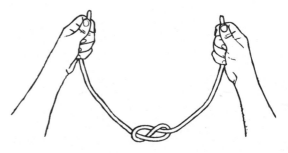

9. As you pull your hands apart, the knot will roll off your left arm.

The Real Don't Let Go

This is supposedly an ancient trick, as demonstrated in the fiction story in the introduction of the book. It is the only way an Overhand can be tied into a rope without *really* letting go.

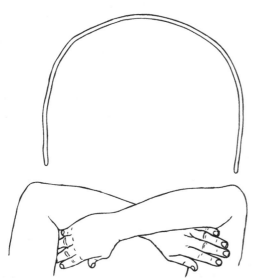

1. Lay the rope down and cross your hands as shown.

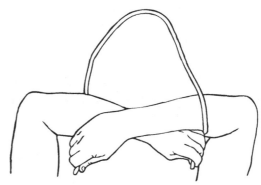

2. Pick up each end of the rope. Notice as you pick it up with your left hand you will have to reach over your right arm to pick up the end.

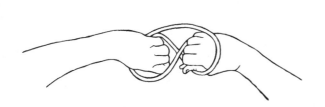

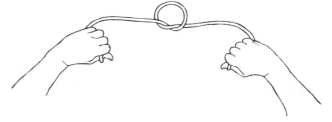

3. Unfold your arms and the knot will fall into the rope.

The Jerry Stone Pop A Knot

My good friend Jerry Stone came up with a way to cheat when popping a knot. He never had the patience to learn my tricks.

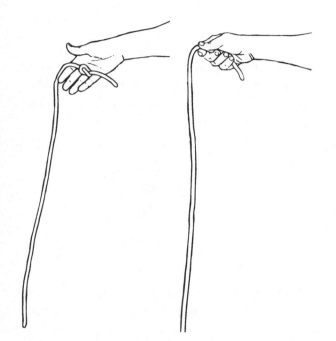

1. He first tied a knot and hid it in his hand.

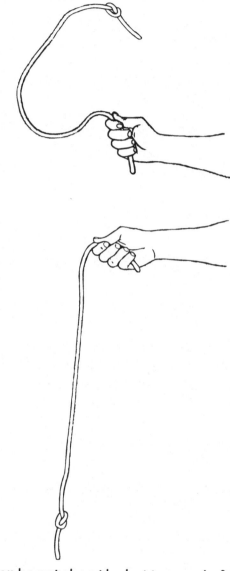

3. Then he catches the bottom end of the rope and lets the knotted end fall giving the appearance that he "popped" the knot. That Jerry Stone...

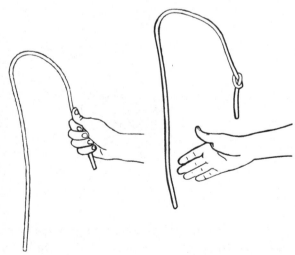

2. As he brings his hand up, he lets the rope fly out of his hand.

Thread The Needle

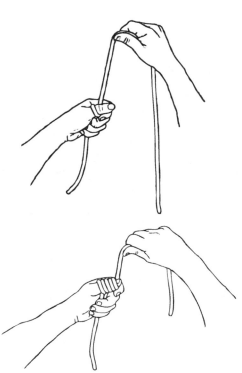

3. Lightly pinch the loop between your thumb and index finger. Explain that this is the eye of the needle, and that usually the eye of a needle is very small.

1. Wrap the rope around your thumb. The number of wraps is not crucial. Tell your audience that this is the "needle."

4. Pull the end of the rope coming from the underhand loop until the loop is very small.

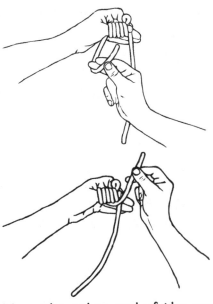

2. Make an underhand loop as shown. An underhand loop has the working end behind the standing end.

5. Hold up the other end of the rope, explaining that it is the thread. As you have everyone's attention focused on this end, you also tuck the rope under your thumb.

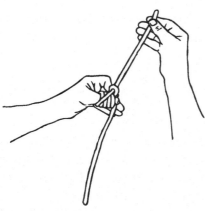

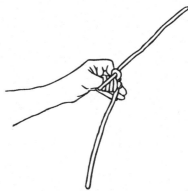

6. Now explain that you are going to throw the thread through the eye. Take the end quickly over the loop, continuing past until the rope tucked under your thumb slides into the loop from underneath.

7. Then quickly drop the end of the rope making it appear as though you have thrown the end through the loop.

You can further baffle people by tying a large knot in the end of the rope and throwing it through the loop. Or even more impressive would be to tie a weighted object to the end of the rope such as keys, a carabiner, a coffee cup, or a water bottle.

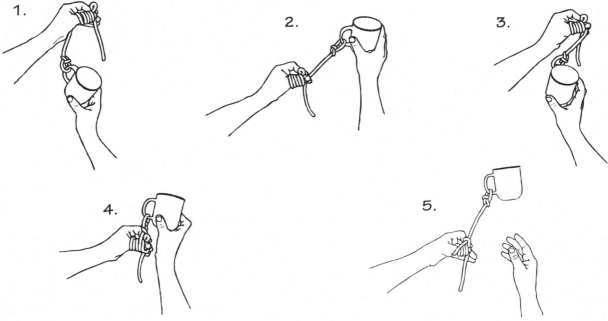

With weighted objects, just throw the object over your hand and the weight will cause the rope to slide into the loop once it stops. Before you throw the object, make sure to tuck the rope attached to it under your thumb as above.

Rope (Eskimo) Yo-Yo

This trick has a rich history in the far north. A true Eskimo yo-yo is made from a piece of leather, rope, or string with weighted (sometimes artistic) objects sewn on each end. I learned it with just a rope.

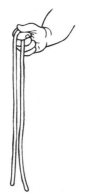

1. Hold the rope around your index finger.

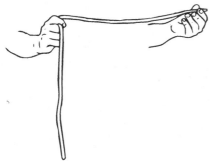

2. Pick up the end coming out on top with your left hand and hold it off to the side.

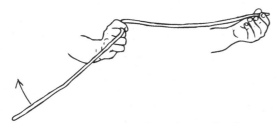

3. Swing your right hand until the end hanging down begins to spin counter-clockwise in a circle. Keep the rope spinning in counter-clockwise circles by moving your right hand up and down, not in a circular motion. Move your hand up when the rope is on the way up, and down when the rope is on the way down.

4. Once you can maintain the spinning rope just by up and down movements of the hand, you are ready for the next step. This step is all about timing. When the rope in motion is on its way up, take the rope in your left hand and send it up at the same time with enough momentum that it to can begin to spin in a clockwise motion.

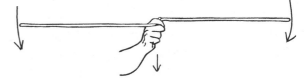

5. Keep both ropes spinning in opposite directions by moving your right hand down on the downward spins and up on the upward spins.

This trick takes a lot of practice for some people (I was one); but once mastered, you can keep both ropes spinning in opposite directions for a long time. Occasionally, the ropes will hit each other and you have to start over. Once you have it down, another trick is to go from an up-and-down motion with your hand to a side-to-side motion while keeping the ropes spinning in opposite directions.

Tom Fool Knot

The Tom Fool knot is basically a Bow-Knot tied in a manner that is difficult for a spectator to duplicate. I am sure many wagers have been lost on this trick. I have learned about four ways of tying the knot, some more difficult to follow than others. This is one that I particularly like; however, it's good to know several methods. You can switch methods to cause more confusion.

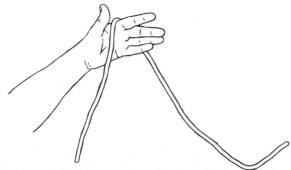

1. Lay the rope on your left hand as in the drawing, with ten inches or more hanging down below your hand.

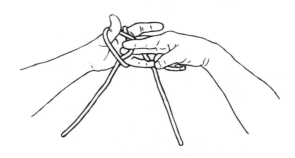

3. With your right hand, reach through the bight of rope on your thumb and grab the rope on your palm with the index finger and middle finger of the right hand.

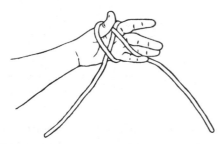

2. Continue to wrap the rope around your hand and up over your thumb, and tuck the rope between your ring finger and little finger.

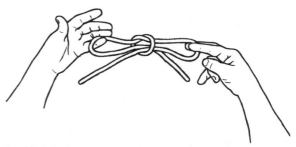

4. Hold onto both ropes and pull your hands apart.

Practice until you can tie the knot smoothly in about two seconds. Then you are ready to see if someone can or cannot duplicate the knot. Most people don't catch that you are pinching the rope and pulling with the left hand fingers because the right hand hides this move. Once the knot is tied, I immediately either lay it in my palms for inspection or hold it with a different set of fingers...

Knotted Bow

This trick starts with a Tom Fool Knot (see previous trick). I will show a different method of tying the knot so that you will have two methods. If knot tying becomes a hobby, I am sure you will learn other methods.

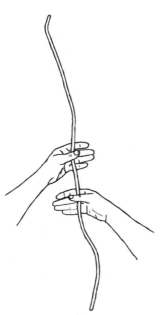

1. Hold the rope as shown.

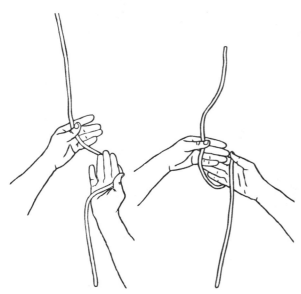

2. Bring the fingers on your right hand over the rope between your hands and under your left hand as shown.

3. Pinch the rope coming out from your left thumb between your right index finger and middle fingers and hold on. Then pinch the rope lying on your right palm between your left index finger and middle finger. Hold on.

4. Then pull both hands apart while holding on with your fingers. You now have a Tom Fool Knot. Pull the knot snug. This is important for later in the trick.

5. When you are first learning this trick, it's probably a good idea to lay the knot down so that it looks exactly like the drawing above. Notice that the working end on the right is on top of the knot, while the working end on the left is on the bottom of the knot. This is also important.

6. Now drop the working end on the right through the bight on the right.

7. Then take the working end on the left toward you and down through the top of the left bight. This trick will not work if you bring the ends through the bights in any other pattern.

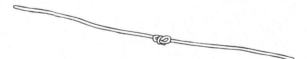

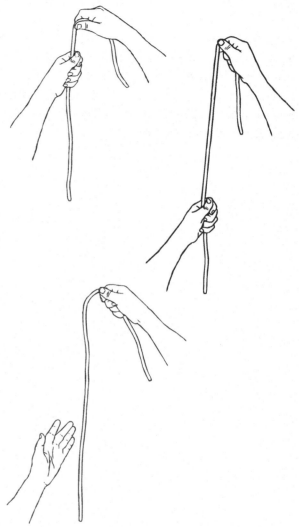

8. Pull both ends until the bights constrict and make a knot. If you did everything right, you can continue to pull and the knot will fall apart. To make the trick a good presentation, you can stop pulling when the knot forms as above. You can even give a few false pulls to make it look like a snug knot. If the knot falls apart too easily, tie the knot again and make sure you pull the Tom Fool Knot tighter before dropping the ends through the bights.

9. Now you can hold the knot in one hand as you give a few tugs on either end of the rope, and then pretend to slide the knot off the end of the rope. Of course, while you're tugging the ends of the rope, the knot falls apart in you hand.

With children, I often pretend to put the knot in my pocket. Inevitably a child asks to see the knot. If so, I reach back in my pocket and pull out a Double Overhand that I tied on a short piece of rope and placed in my pocket beforehand.

Sniff A Rope

This is a two-person trick. Both people have to know the secret.

Start by asking your friend (who is in on the trick) to leave the area. Next, hold the rope horizontally with each hand holding an end. Then ask someone to touch the rope at any place. Explain that your friend is going to come in and smell the rope to find the exact location the rope has been touched. Call your friend back. Hold the rope horizontally at about waist height as your friend starts at one end of the rope and smells his or her way down to the other.

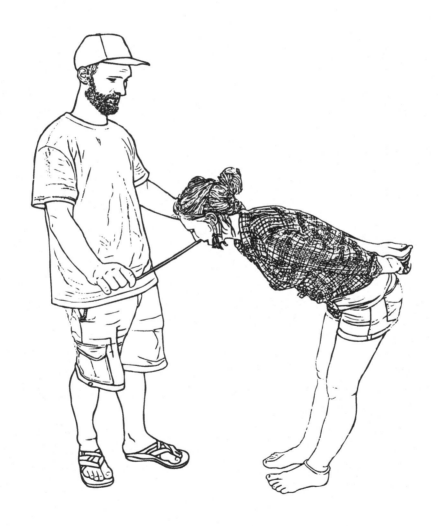

As your friend gets to the spot that was touched, wiggle your toe just enough for your friend to notice. Your friend who knows to be watching for the wiggle will stop and point to the spot. Of course spectators are watching the person smelling the rope, not the feet of the person holding the rope.

Ghost Fingers

Ghost finger tricks give the impression that the rope penetrates through the fingers. These are fun tricks to demonstrate and then see if someone can duplicate what you just did. These were obviously devised by people who had a lot of time on their hands. Most of these tricks work best with a three-foot long rope or string tied in a loop. The Square Knot is a good knot to use to tie the ends together. Here are some I have collected over the years.

Old Sailor's Ghost Fingers

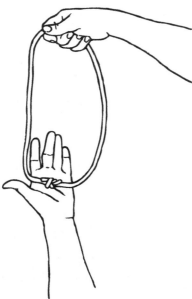

1. Lay the loop of rope over your left hand as shown, with the knot lying in the palm of your hand.

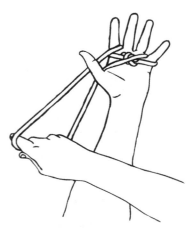

3. Wrap the ropes around the left side of your left thumb. As you do this, notice which rope is on top.

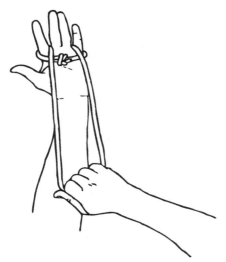

2. Pull the bight of rope from below up and between your fingers as shown. Make sure to hold your right hand as shown. You never have to reposition your right hand on the rope—just turn your wrist to position the rope as shown in the drawings.

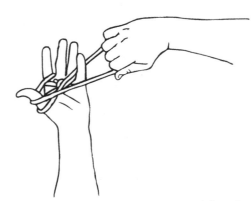

4. Next, cross the ropes and hook your left little finger.

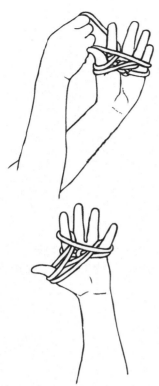

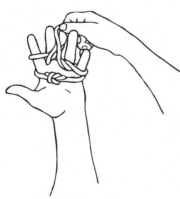

5. Then loop the rope around your index finger.

6. Take both bights off your thumb and lay them between your ring finger and middle finger.

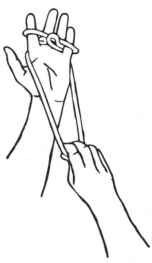

7. At this point you have a big mess on your hand. Grab the rope at the knot and pull towards you.

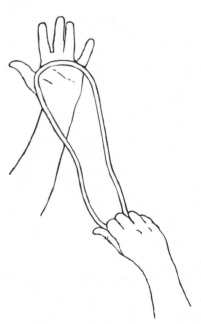

8. If you did everything right, the rope should appear to penetrate the fingers. If you made just one mistake, the rope will not fall off your hand.

Figure Eight Ghost Fingers

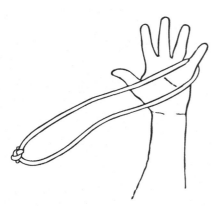

1. Place the middle of the rope on you little finger.

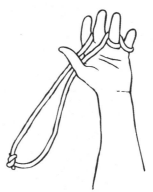

3. Repeat the process for each of your fingers as you work toward your thumb.

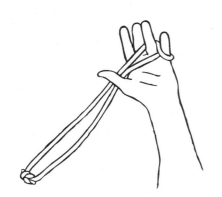

2. Twist the rope to form a loop around your little finger as you lay the rope over your ring finger.

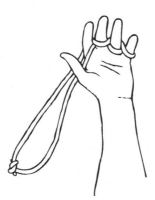

4. Notice that the same rope ends up on top all the way across your fingers.

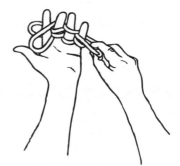

7. Pull your thumb out from the loops.

5. Wrap both ropes around your thumb with out crossing the ropes.

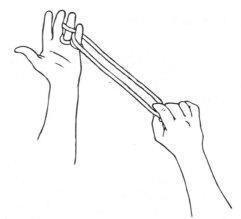

8. Pull the knotted ends down.

6. Figure-eight the rope back to your little finger. On the way back, the rope that was on the top the first way is on the bottom as you return. It should also be on the same side of each finger.

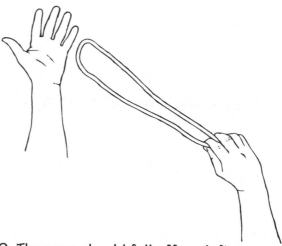

9. The rope should fall off each finger.

Double Figure Eight Ghost Fingers

This trick requires a much larger loop. Make the loop out of a six-foot length of string or rope with the ends tied together in a square knot.

1. Hook your two little fingers in the loop.

2. Hook each adjacent finger in the loop by going over the top string and into the back of the loop.

3. This will cause the loop to figure eight the rope around your fingers on both hands simultaneously.

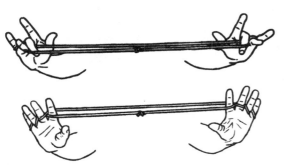

4. Continue this process with each finger working towards your thumbs.

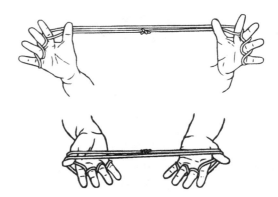

5. Turn your hands inward causing the ropes to wrap around your thumbs. Notice the ropes do not cross.

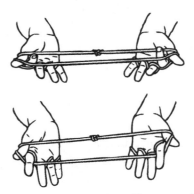

6. Next, poke your index fingers directly through the front of the loop.

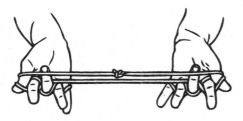

7. Then your middle finger will come under the bottom rope and through the back of the loop.

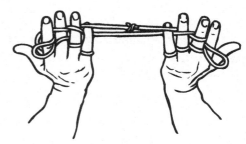

9. Now both hands are tied up in figure-eights. Hold your fingertips up and pull your thumbs out of the loops.

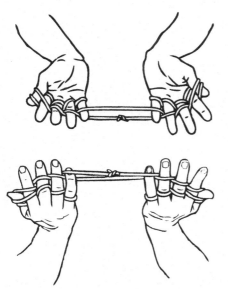

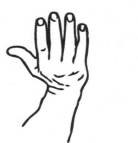

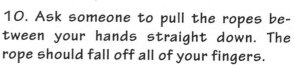

10. Ask someone to pull the ropes between your hands straight down. The rope should fall off all of your fingers.

8. As you straighten your fingers out, the rope will figure-eight around your fingers. Follow the same procedure all the way back to your little finger.

Captain Hook's Ghost Finger

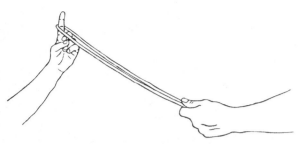

1. Place a bight in the rope over another person's index finger, and hold both ends of the rope with your left hand.

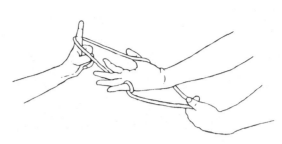

4. Then slide your thumb under the other rope.

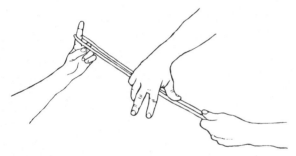

2. Take your right hand over both ropes and hook the far rope from underneath with your little finger.

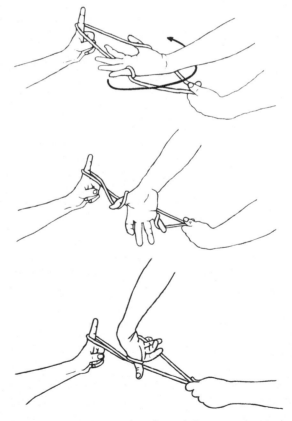

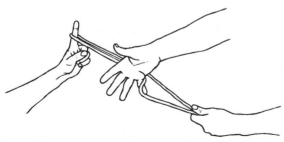

3. Flip your right hand to the palm up position causing a loop to form around your little finger.

5. Move your right hand in a counter-clockwise motion, keeping your palm up as far as possible following the arrow.

6. Once you make the full rotation, place your little finger on the other person's index finger.

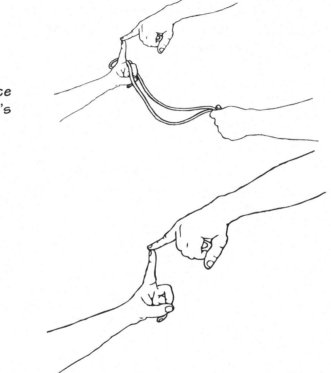

7. Drop the bight off your thumb and pull the two ends of rope toward you. It may help to slightly raise your right hand while your little finger stays on their index finger.

8. The rope will appear to penetrate their index finger!

Spinning Hand Ghost Finger

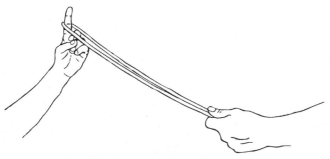

1. Place a bight in the rope over your participant's index finger. Hold both ends of the rope with your left hand.

2. Take your right hand over both ropes and hook the far rope from underneath with your middle finger.

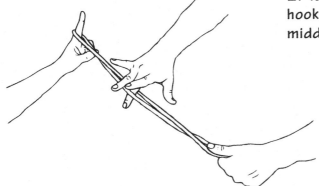

3. Twist your hand into the upright position causing the rope to figure-eight.

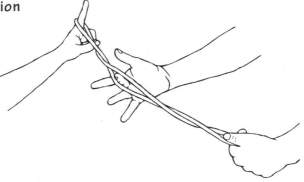

4. keep your finger in between the ropes and flip your hand so that your palm is facing up as in the drawing.

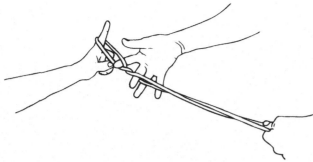

5. Put your index finger in the top loop of the figure-eight.

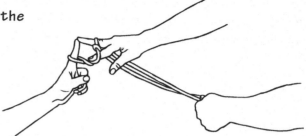

6. Twist your hand back around until your middle finger can come to rest on top of your participant's index finger. Notice that your index finger hooks the rope as your hand twists back around.

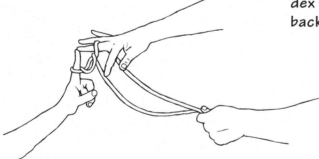

7. Drop the bight off your index finger and pull the two ends of rope toward you. It may help to slightly raise your right hand while your middle finger stays on their index finger.

8. The rope will appear to penetrate their index finger.

Gun Point Ghost Finger

1. Place a bight in the rope over your participant's index finger as shown. Notice the rope has a twist in it, with the working end on the left on top.

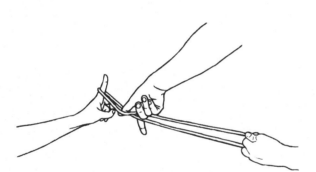

2. Place the thumb of your right hand in the top loop of the figure-eight, and your index finger in the lower loop as in the drawing.

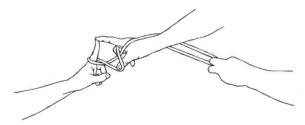

3. Twist your hand and place your index finger on your participant's index finger. Notice that you hook a bight with your thumb as you twist your hand.

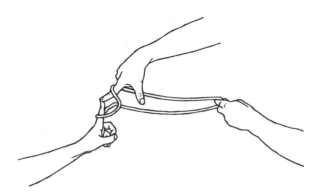

4. Drop the bight off your thumb and pull the two ends of rope toward you. It may help to slightly raise your right hand while your index finger stays on their index finger.

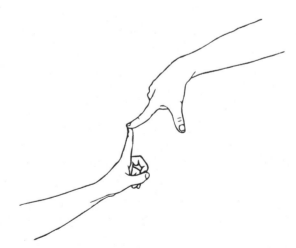

5. The rope will appear to penetrate their index finger!

Strangled Ghost Finger

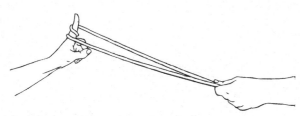

1. Wrap a loop of rope over your participant's index finger.

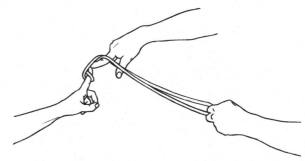

4. Pull lightly on the two ends of the rope as you raise your right hand. Make sure to keep your index finger on their finger the whole time.

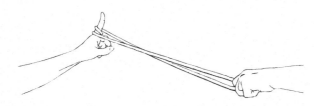

2. Twist the rope once causing the rope to figure-eight, and hold both ends of the rope with your left hand. The end of rope on the left side should be on top.

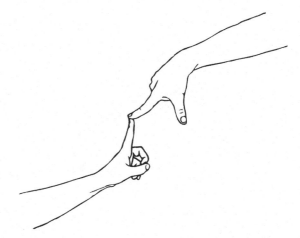

5. The rope will appear to penetrate their index finger! For added effect, blow on the rope right before it drops off.

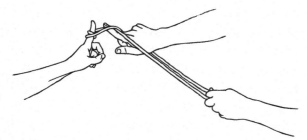

3. Take your right index finger down through the lower loop of the figure-eight and up through the top loop. Place your index finger on their index finger.

Ghost Thumb

The illusion for this trick is that you will wrap a loop around your own thumb and pull the loop though your thumb.

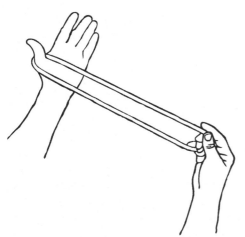

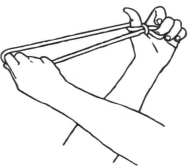

3. Take the loop that your right Index finger is poking through and turn it upside down, placing it over your thumb.

1. Place a bight of rope on your left thumb. Hold both ends with your right hand exactly as shown in drawing so that there is space between the two ends.

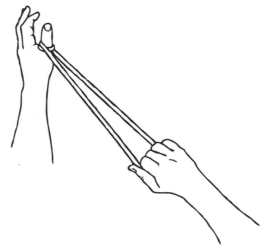

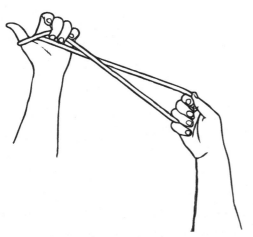

4. As the rope snugs up against your thumb, slowly remove your left middle finger from the bight. Two bights should catch each other behind your thumb. Maintain light pressure on your thumb so that the two bights hold together. You can hide the two locking bights behind your thumb so that the rope appears to be wrapped around your thumb.

2. Reach across both ropes and hook the outer one with your left middle finger. Pull this rope across the other, forming a figure-eight.

With a strong pull from your right hand, the rope will appear to pop through your thumb!

Square Knot Cut And Restore

This trick is preformed best with a piece of string about six feet long.

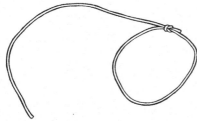

1. Take the middle of your string and one of the working ends, and tie a Square Knot. You should have a large loop in half of your rope.

4. Pull hard on the two ends, explaining that the Square Knot is a good knot. As you pull, the knot will actually 'pop' into a Larks Head Knot. This knot can slide on the string. If your ends are too short, the piece of string will 'pop' off the standing part. Practice will help you learn exactly how long the ends should be to keep them attached when pulling the string tight.

2. Cut the rope with a knife or scissors next to the square knot as shown, next to where the working end comes out of the knot.

5. Wrap the string onto your left hand. As the knot gets into your right hand, it will be concealed. Continue to hold onto the knot as you wrap the rest of the string onto your left hand. You will be able to slide the knot off the end of the string, keeping it concealed in your right hand.

Hold your left hand out and ask someone to tap on your left hand three times. This creates a diversion while you put the knot in your pocket.

3. If you take a close look, you have only cut off the end of the rope, although it appears the rope is cut in half.

Have someone else hold the end of the string that's sticking out of your hand as you slowly unwrap the string from your left hand. The string is restored!

Double Loop Cut And Restore

This trick is performed with a piece of string about six feet long. Tie the two ends of the string together to make a large loop.

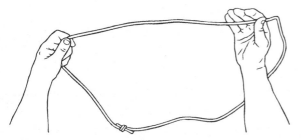

1. Hold the loop exactly as shown.

The next step is to twist the loop in order to make a double loop. As I am doing this, I usually say something like, "two loops are better than one." The twisting action is the key to the trick. Follow the directions carefully.

2. A half twist makes a double loop. You want to make a full twist as shown in the diagram.

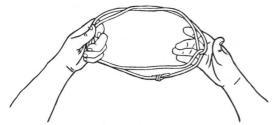

3. When you make a full twist, two interlocking bights form. As you pull your hands apart make sure to conceal the two interlocking bights in your hand.

4. Have a volunteer cut through both strings with a knife or scissors close to the concealed bights, as shown.

5. It now appears that you have two long strings. Give the two long ends to a volunteer and have them tie the two ends together while you put the short ends in your mouth. Of course, the two short ends are actually just a small bight of string attached to a larger bight.

As the volunteer is tying their two ends together, work the small bight off the large bight with your tongue and tuck it between your cheek and gum.

As the volunteer finishes up, pop the string out of your mouth. The string is restored!

This trick is best performed with a piece of string about six feet long. I usually allow someone to inspect the string before starting.

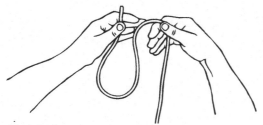

1. Hold the string near the end with one hand while you pick up the middle of the rope with the thumb and index finger of your other hand.

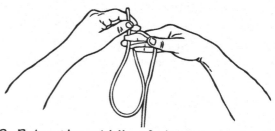

2. Bring the middle of the rope up to the left hand. As you approach the left hand, pinch the string with your right index and middle fingers, as shown.

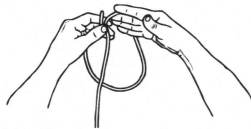

3. Immediately drop the string from your right thumb and pull it up with your right index and middle fingers. This move creates two interlocking bights that can be concealed in your left hand.

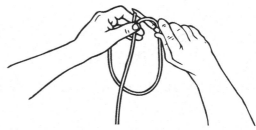

4. Have a volunteer cut the string with a knife or scissors as shown. It appears that the string has been cut in half. In reality, only an inch or so has been cut from the end of the string.

5. There are two ways to "restore" the rope at this point (or get rid of the end piece). One method is to place the two short ends in your mouth as you give one of each of the long ends to volunteers. Work the bight loose in your mouth and tuck it between your cheek and gum. As you are doing this, you can signal to the volunteers to begin pulling on their ends of the string. Drop the string out of your mouth. The string is restored!

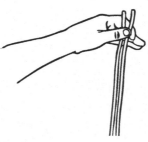

The second method is to tie the two short ends together in a tight Overhand Knot around the standing part of the long string. This will give the appearance that you tied two ends of string together. You actually tied an Overhand Knot that can slide on the string. Wrap the string around your hand as you slide the Overhand Knot off. Have someone unwrap the string from your hand as you tuck the knot away in your pocket.

Thief Knot

The Thief Knot is so named because it appears to be a Square Knot on first glance, but it falls apart when put to the test. The story I have heard about its origin is that a cook on a sailing vessel suspected that members of the crew were sneaking food from his food bags in the middle of the night. To find out if his suspicion was true, he tied all his food bags in Thief Knots. Upon his return the next day, the bags were tied in Square Knots. Someone had been getting into the food!

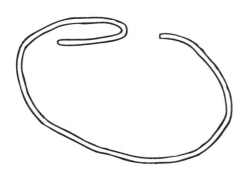

1. Start with a bight in one end of the rope.

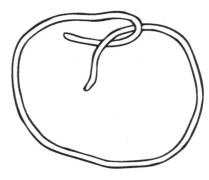

2. Pass the other end up through the bight as shown.

3. Now pass under the two ends of the bight starting with the working end side of the bight.

4. Pass back down through the bight.

You now have a bight on a bight with the working ends on opposite sides. The difference in the Square Knot and the Thief Knot is where the ends come out of the knots. The ends of the Thief Knot come out on opposite sides. The ends of the Square Knot come out on the same side.

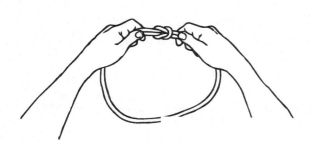

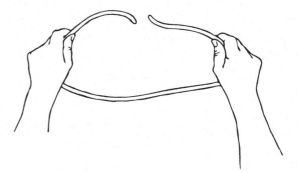

5. If you hold the knot as shown above, it appears that you have just tied a Square Knot. Even an expert knot tier would not know unless they could see the ends.

6. Give a good strong pull on the two ends, and the knot will fall apart.

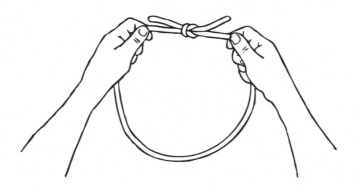

The knot above is a Square Knot. You will not be able to pull this knot apart.

You can play a trick on someone who knows how to tie a Square Knot but not the Thief Knot. Both of you should have a small rope. Ask them to tie a Square Knot. You tie a Thief Knot in your rope while they are tying the Square Knot in theirs. Hold your Thief Knot with both hands covering the working ends, and ask them to compare their knot with yours. Ask if they agree that you both have Square Knots. You can even flip the knot over and let them examine it with the back of their knot. Once agreed, ask them to pull on the two standing ends as you do the same. Your knot will pull apart, and the Square Knot will tighten down.

Dragon Bowline

This trick is a more of a play on words than a trick. I have found it to be a fun way to trick someone who thinks they really know their knots! I start off by saying that I learned a special knot from the Japanese. It's in the Bowline family. There are all kinds of bowlines: Double Bowline, Bowline on a Bight, Bowline on a Coil, Spanish Bowline... This special knot is a Dragon Bowline.

Take a rope or string about six feet long and tie a Bowline at the end. Then throw it on the ground and begin dragging the Bowline across the floor by the other end. There you have it – the dragging (dragon) Bowline...

Binder's Twine Twist

I learned this trick while working with horses. The hay was bundled together with binder's twine. The trick only works with binder's twine made of natural material. This type of binder's twine is actually many small pieces of natural fiber that are twisted together intermittently to create strong cordage. Take about a six-foot length of twine and ask someone to attempt to break it. Once they give up, tell them that binder's twine is not that strong. It can't even hold up a brick or small rock!

Tie one end of the binder's twine to a tree branch. Then tie the brick or small rock to the other end and let it hang.

It appears that you were wrong, but wait. The binder's twine will begin to slowly untwist. In a matter of minutes it will break, sending the brick or rock to the ground.

Section III:

Tricks For Young Children

Young children (two to eight years old) typically have more active imaginations than older children or adults. Therefore, they are more gullible for simple tricks. These tricks are for young children. Most children this age do not have the coordination to perform the tricks. Never leave young children unattended with ropes, and never let them put ropes around their necks.

Blow A Knot

This trick can be performed with about three feet of rope.

1. Tie a Slip Knot in the middle of the rope. Pull the knot snug.

2. Pull the two ends until the knot constricts and is ready to fall apart.
Stop at this point. The rope is ready for the trick.

Ask a child to blow on the knot. As she does, pull on the two ends to cause the knot to disappear.

You can add to this trick by tying three Slip Knots. Pull each knot until the bight is drawn in. One knot should be in the middle of the rope, and one close to each end.
Hold the two end knots in your hands, hiding them. Ask the child to blow on the knot. As she does, pull on the two ends to cause the knot in the middle to disappear. Next you can open up your right hand in amazement that the knot traveled to the end of the rope.

Ask the child to blow on that knot and pull as she does. Open up your left hand in amazement that the knot has now traveled to the other end. Ask the child to blow on that knot, and pull as the knot finally disappears for good!

Chain Sinnet

This trick can be performed with a rope three to six feet long.

1. Tie a Slip Knot in one end of the rope.

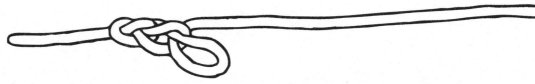

2. Reach through the bight and pull a bight of the standing part through the Slip Knot.

3. Continue the process until you are at the end of the rope.

Then hold on to one end of the rope and ask a child to pull on the other. To his amazement, the whole thing will disappear.

This knot is called the Chain Sinnet. Electricians will sometimes tie up their cords with this knot for storage because it is easily untied.

If you do this with a Chain Sinnet, it's useful to know that you can pull the end through the last Slip Knot to secure the knot. Then simply pull the end out when you are ready to untie the whole thing. If it's a long rope or cord, you can tie a Slip Knot or even another Chain Sinnet with the chain-plaited rope or cord.

Ghost Arm

Like the Ghost Fingers, this trick will give the illusion that you are cutting the rope through the child's arm. The trick requires a three to five-foot rope with the ends tied together to form a loop.

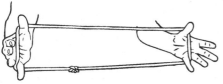

1. Hold the rope between your hands with the rope threaded over your fingers as shown in the drawing.

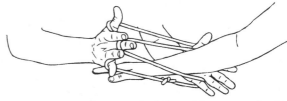

3. Ask the child to hold up his arm. As he does, slide the rope around his arm as shown.

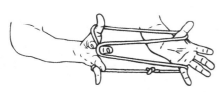

2. Then reach your right hand over to the left and pick up the rope on your left hand with your right middle finger. Pull your hands apart with the rope still on your middle finger as in the drawing.

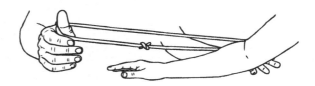

4. Drop the rope off your left-hand little finger and pull your hands apart. It will appear to the child that the loop penetrated his arm. For added effect, before dropping the bight off my little finger, I will move both hands up and down causing the child's arm to bounce up and down against the ropes. Then on my last upward swing, I release the bight from my little finger as I pull my thumbs apart.

Continuous Loop

Hide the two ends of a three-foot rope in your left hand. Place a bight of rope in your mouth. While doing so, tell the child you are placing the ends of the rope in your mouth. Pretend to weave the ends together in your mouth, and then pull the rope out. It will appear that the rope is a continuous loop. Continue holding the two ends tightly with your left hand. Slide the right hand several times across the rope beside your left hand, giving the impression that you are sliding the loop of rope around and around.

Most of the tricks in this book have their roots in an era that was much less cluttered than our lives today. I like them because they are such a simple form of entertainment. It's fun to master the skills to tie knots quickly and efficiently. There's even some sense of satisfaction in just knowing what knot to use for a given situation.

As for the tricks just for fun in part two of this book, I enjoy these for the interaction it brings between people. It's fun knowing how to do something that others don't. However, much of the fun comes from watching others eventually figure out what you are doing—the "secret" to the trick.

There is a dilemma for the trickster, however. Do you show the secret, or let them struggle to figure it out on their own? If you show the secret too soon, they will miss out on the fun that comes with figuring it out on their own. I have found that in most cases people who figure tricks out on their own appreciate the tricks much more than those who have been shown the secret. However, after a certain amount of attempts some people will begin to get frustrated, or maybe even angry. The fun is lost. If this continues, the admiration for the trickster is lost as well. In fact, you may even look more like a jerk.

I want to give you some advice on rope trick etiquette that comes from years of experience and observation. Keeping and making friends is way more important than showing off how great you are. If you are sharing a rope trick with someone and they get to the point where it no longer looks like they are having fun, help them out. Encourage them, give them a hint, or even share the secret. Then everyone is having fun—not just you.

Ashley, Clifford W. *The Ashley Book of Knots*. London: Faber and Faber, 1988. Print.

Budworth, Geoffrey. *The Knot Book*. New York: Sterling, 1985. Print.

Budworth, Geoffrey. *The Ultimate Encyclopedia of Knots & Ropework*. London: Southwater, 2009. Print.

Day, Cyrus Lawrence, Ray O. Beard, and M. Lee. Hoffman. *The Art of Knotting & Splicing*. Annapolis, MD: Naval Institute, 1986. Print.

Fulves, Karl, and Joseph K. Schmidt. *Self-working Rope Magic: 70 Foolproof Tricks*. New York: Dover Publications, 1990. Print.

Gibson, Walter Brown, and Walter Brown Gibson. *The Complete Guide to Knots and How to Tie Them*. Hollywood, FL: Lifetime, 1997. Print.

James, Stewart. *Abbott's Encyclopedia of Rope Tricks for Magicians*. New York: Dover Publications, 1975. Print.

Leeming, Joseph. *Fun with String; a Collection of String Games, Useful Braiding & Weaving, Knot Work & Magic with String and Rope*. New York: Dover Publications, 1974. Print.

Macfarlan, Allan A., and Paulette Jumeau Macfarlan. *Knotcraft; the Art of Knot Tying*. New York: Association, 1967. Print.

Tarbell, Harlan, Ralph W. Read, Bruce Elliott, Harry Lorayne, and Ed Mishell. *The Tarbell Course in Magic*. New York: L. Tannen, 1943. Print.

Tarbell, Harlan. *The Tarbell Course in Magic: Volume 3 (lessons 34 to 45)*. New York: Louis Tannen, 1977. Print.

Turner, J. C., and Pieter Van De Griend. *History and Science of Knots*. Singapore: World Scientific, 1996. Print.

Made in the USA
Coppell, TX
17 November 2022